LORRAINE PETERSON was born in Red Wing, Minnesota, grew up on a farm near Ellsworth, Wisconsin, and now resides in Ciudad Juárez, Mexico. She received her B.A. (in history) from North Park College in Chicago, and has taken summer courses from the University of Minnesota and the University of Mexico in Mexico City.

Lorraine has taught high school and junior high. She has been an advisor to nondenominational Christian clubs in Minneapolis public schools, has taught teenage Bible studies, and continues to work with young people. She has written several bestselling devotional books for teens:

Anybody Can Be Cool, But Awesome Takes Practice
Dying of Embarrassment & Living to Tell About It
Falling Off Cloud Nine and Other High Places
If God Loves Me, Why Can't I Get My Locker Open?
If the Devil Made You Do It, You Blew It!
If You Really Trust Me, Why Can't I Stay Out Later?
Lord, I Haven't Talked to You Since the Last Crisis, But ...
Please Give Me Another Chance, Lord
Radical Advice From the Ultimate Wise Guy
Real Characters in the Making
Trying to Get Toothpaste Back Into the Tube
Why Isn't God Giving Cash Prizes?

Lord, I Haven't Talked to You Since the Last Crisis, But...

Lord, I Haven't Talked to You Since the Last Crisis, But...

LORRAINE PETERSON

BETHANY HOUSE PUBLISHERS
MINNEAPOLIS, MINNESOTA 55438

Illustrations by Paula Becker

Published by Bethany House Publishers
A Ministry of Bethany Fellowship, Inc.
11300 Hampshire Avenue South
Minneapolis, Minnesota 55438

Printed in the United States of America.

Library of Congress Cataloging-in-Publication Data

Peterson, Lorraine.
    Lord, I haven't talked to you since the last crisis, but— / Lorraine Peterson
        p.   cm.
    1. Teenagers—Prayer-books and devotions—English.
[1. Prayer books and devotions.] I. Title.
BV4850.P4625   1994
242'.63—dc20   93–40579
ISBN 1–55661–385–7   CIP

Preface

If this book convinces even one reader to establish the habit of daily devotions, and to devote a lifetime to making friends with God, I will consider it the most important book I've ever written.

Why do I believe this is so urgent? Just take a look around.

Today, every one of us faces a post-Christian society in which biblical principles are hated and challenged every inch of the way. The breakup of the family has hurt many—especially young people. On top of that, our high-pressure culture produces a kind of super-stress that few people can deal with successfully. Besides all this, there seems to be an extreme scarcity of totally-sold-out-to-Jesus role models for us to pattern our lives after. Why? It seems that so many believers are caught up in materialism, status, and pleasure that there's not much time left to really get to know God. Tragically, this type of existence is often passed off as the normal Christian life, and so young people—and older people alike—get the idea that Christianity is merely a subculture instead of a willingness to obey God no matter how much it costs.

Then we wonder why friendless kids turn away from churches and join gangs just because they need to belong. Others seek spiritual experiences in Eastern or New Age meditation. More lose themselves in video games, MTV, or occultic rituals. And many teenagers who have scriptural training and know how to avoid all these snares never really make their lives count for Christ. The majority are only playing a type of "defensive ball game"—they want to be Christian enough to escape hell, but they don't see any personal advantage in winning others to the Lord.

I feel strongly that one of the keys to changing this situation is for the Christian young person to develop a strong devotional life. Making friends with God is, after all, the only way to live life in a different dimension. As 2 Peter 1:3–4 says:

His divine power has given us everything we need for life and godliness through our knowledge of him who called us by his own glory and goodness. Through these he has given us his very great and precious promises, so that through them you may participate in the divine nature and escape the corruption in the world caused by evil desires.

Everything we need is available to us—but the resources we have in Christ aren't being tapped. Amid all the things that are recommended to help today's young people, we tend to forget that a daily appointment with the One who is called "Wonderful Counselor" is available to everyone. And it doesn't cost a cent. Instead of the frantic pursuit of pleasure or chemical escape, there is always the chance for inner renewal by spending time with the one Person who understands every need completely and is equipped with the power to do something about each situation. Those moments spent alone with God will reorganize priorities to the point that life ceases to be hopelessly hectic. Letting God's Word and prayer melt harmful things like bitterness and tension will release love and infuse hope that gives a new outlook on life.

I feel that if the structure for quiet time alone with God is not firmly in place, we have no anchor for the storms that are sure to come. If we don't know how to receive from God in a meaningful way, there is no place to turn when parents, peers, or church groups fail to meet our needs. Only getting inspiration, correction, doctrine, and security directly from studying the Scriptures and spending quality time with God can produce purpose, conviction, and stability in our lives. I'm convinced that no one can have a rock-solid relationship with Christ without setting aside a special time to meet with Him each day and effectively using that time.

Therefore, the "generation at risk," the kids whose lives are filled with confusion and emptiness, must be presented with what I consider the most workable solution to the cumulating chaos—seeking God with a sincere heart, personally studying and absorbing His Word, and taking the time to sit in His presence, talking life over with Him and listening to His answers.

This book encourages young people to make the time to be alone with God. It provides some teaching on the just-between-you-and-God aspects of prayer, and gives a lot of different suggestions about what to do on a "date with God." (I don't discuss the big topic of intercession for others because I will deal with that in another volume.)

I'd like to thank my friends and family for their help and support as I've written this book. My roommate, Maria Teresa Rodriquez, helped me pray for this book, and put up with my usually messy office that doubles as our TV room. My sister, Lynn, and my brother-in-law, Earl, along with my nieces and nephews Beth, Brett, Kaari, and Kirk—as usual—gave me constructive comments and encouragement. Without the help of my talented and understanding editor David Hazard, this book may have never come off the press. My long-time friend Jewell Erickson sent me just the book I needed to continue writing when I'd reached a dead end. Then Aida, a friend from church, gave me a book on tape that helped me finish the chapter I'd planned. I always marvel at God's faithfulness and timing. Obviously, He deserves *all* the credit for getting this project finished.

Several books especially influenced this one: *Ordering Your Private World* by Gordon MacDonald; *Enjoying the Closeness of God* by Roger C. Palms; *How to Listen to God* by Charles Stanley; *Hudson Taylor's Spiritual Secret* by Dr. and Mrs. Howard Taylor; *Listening to God,* by Joyce Huggett; *The Prayer Factor* by Sammy Tippit; and *Seven Guides to Effective Prayer* by Colin Whittaker.

Contents

Section 1:   It's About Your Attitude—Maybe You've
              Grown Up, But Your Prayers Haven't!

1. Making Friends With God 15
2. "I Just Need to Talk to Somebody" 23
3. Before the Roof Caves In 37
4. Are Your Actions Making You a Stranger to
   the One Who Loves You Most? 53
5. Troubled Teen Survival Kit 69
6. Pray With Your Life 85

Section 2:   Just Between God and Me: Parts of Prayer

7. Is "Thank You" Part of Your Vocabulary? 105
8. When 911 Prayers Just Won't Do the Job 121
9. Pizza With Bill, Irregular Verbs, and Spring Break 147
10. But That's Not What I Want to Hear 171
11. God, If I Were Running Your Universe 195
12. Out of Focus 219

1

It's About Your Attitude— Maybe You've Grown Up, But Your Prayers Haven't!

Chapter One
Making Friends With God

☑ But This Is Important—I Can Hang Out With God Anytime

The Ballantyne family had moved again. But that was nothing new. Robbie's father was in the Air Force and he'd lived all over the country. Although he hated having to be the new kid again, what he heard about the high school he'd be attending pleased him.

Lakeview High was famous for its winning football teams, had a fine coaching staff, and was a small school—so maybe Robbie would have a chance. Clumsy, lacking in self-confidence, and only an average athlete, Robbie, nevertheless, cherished a dream: He wanted to be a football hero. Going into the ninth grade in a setting like Lakeview— and with the security that his family was scheduled to stay put for four years—was more than Robbie had hoped for.

Things were definitely taking a turn for the better. When the Ballantynes moved into their new house, Robbie's mother discovered that their next-door neighbors were also Christians. She invited them over for dinner, and afterward Robbie got a chance to get acquainted with Scott Westfield. Scott was captain of Lakeview's football team, which nearly blew Robbie's mind. He eagerly devoured all the training tips and physical fitness advice that Scott offered.

Scott was also president of the church youth group and was planning to lead a Bible study for ninth-grade boys who attended Lakeview High. When asked if he'd like to join, Robbie enthusiastically accepted. Imagine starting in a new school as a friend of the captain of the football team! He could hardly wait.

The first day of classes was fabulous. Robbie walked to school with Scott, who gave him a quick tour of the school, plus some inside info about how to get along with certain teachers. Six guys showed up at the first Bible study—three others from Scott and Robbie's church, and two non-Christians. Scott inspired them all to be faithful and to do some recruiting. Robbie offered to make up invitations on his computer and to help in any other way he could.

Within weeks, though, the dream-come-true began to sour. Robbie noticed that Scott was becoming too busy with the popular senior clique to notice him—unless there was work to be done. It was, "Robbie, could you call all the guys to tell them we won't meet for Bible study this week?" Or, "The youth pastor gave us leaders this lesson for all the guys in the Bible study group. Please make copies for everyone." Or, "Jim needs a ride home. See that he gets one." Or, "Collect all the money and order the pizza for Monday night. Pay for mine and I'll repay you when I get some cash." Even when Robbie complimented Scott on how well he'd played in Friday night's game, Scott sure didn't show any interest in a real conversation.

One day, Robbie met Scott in the hall and his new "friend" didn't even say hi. Robbie wondered if the fact that Scott was with a popular guy named Pete had anything to do with it.

Then Scott started dating Marnie, and things got worse. One day, he had the nerve to ask Robbie to run home at lunch hour and get the math paper he'd forgotten! Robbie knew that Scott's only excuse for not going himself was that he planned to eat lunch with Marnie. And though Robbie resented being treated like an errand boy, he did it.

A week later, Robbie saw his name listed as head of the clean-up committee for the big youth group fall festival. Scott hadn't even *asked* him. He really felt used.

That evening Robbie sat down at his computer, wondering why he was claiming that Scott was his best friend. He made a sharp-looking printout that read:

A Real Friend Is...

1. Someone who listens, as well as talks.
2. Someone who gives, as well as receives.
3. Someone who puts himself in the place of the other person.
4. Someone who is faithful even when that demands sacrifice.
5. Someone who is willing to do a favor, as well as ask for one.
6. Someone who enjoys making the other person happy.
7. Someone who appreciates the good qualities of another—and at times mentions that fact.

In a way, he was thinking out loud. And it made him realize: Scott wasn't really his friend. That made him sad.

He desperately wanted Scott's friendship, and he'd done everything he knew to make it happen. But friendship has to go two ways, and Robbie could do nothing to force Scott to reciprocate.

Do you think God might feel the way Robbie does when He thinks about His relationship with you? Are you a person who only prays when you need something? Do you treat God like a candy machine or like a Friend you care about? Do you spend more time drying your hair than you do talking with God?

Taking time out to think things over can help you look at some of the things that characterize true friendship and check whether those traits describe your relationship with God.

A close relationship involves things like: considering your friend's feelings first; being faithful; verbalizing appreciation; sacrificing your own desires sometimes to meet the needs of your friend; and making things right if you have done wrong. Does your relationship with God have any of these dimensions? Do you know how to enjoy His presence and listen to Him? Do you want to do His will and obey Him? Are you faithful—defending Him, even in front of your non-Christian friends? Do you spend a lot of time thanking and praising Him? When you sin against Him, do you confess it immediately? Do you square things with people whom you've wronged, so that there is no uneasiness between you and God?

This book is written to help you learn these things so that your communication with God becomes more than a series of demands, needs, and occasional cries for help. God *does* want us to make requests of Him, but that's not all there is to prayer. Maybe you've been missing out on some of the most fantastic aspects of prayer!

True, it's sometimes difficult to know how to spend time with a God you cannot see—so I'll be offering a variety of suggestions and patterns for communicating with God. Because each person has a different personality and background, some ideas will work for you and some may not. For example, some people can really pour out their hearts while reading a written prayer, and others consider that much too formal and stuffy. Some people can get into praying Scripture verses more easily than others. There are those for whom writing a letter to God is true prayer, while certain individuals get headaches at the thought of trying to pen another composition. I'd ask you, however, to seriously attempt to put each idea into practice, because at some time in the future you may want to use it. This may help you to keep from falling into a rut in your prayer life.

Have you and your best friend ever had a talk that began like this: "Every time we get together we just go to McDonald's. We need a change. Let's do something different"? This can easily happen with you and God. Besides, circumstances change, and that can dictate a change in your prayer priorities. For instance, maybe ingratitude is your biggest problem at the moment, and the major emphasis you need in prayer right now is praise and thanksgiving. Later, a specific problem in relationships with Christians could make you want to shift to praying through the book of Ephesians. Or when your life gets so tense that concentration is difficult, reading a prayer on a specific topic can be most helpful. Or when you're overly busy or upset, it may be that you need to learn to be *still* long enough to enjoy God's presence. No method can rekindle that God-has-first-place-in-my-life love, or remove the communication block caused by unconfessed sin. But new types of prayer can become the means of new blessings.

I invite you to join me in the exciting adventure of making friends with God. He's always there—loving you, wanting to help, waiting for you to make Him the most important Person in your life. It's true that any other friendship you have could one day prove to be heartbreaking, but Jesus will never change. He will never fail you, never stop loving you.

Making friends with God is well worth your time and effort.

OH! I DIDN'T REALIZE YOU DON'T KNOW EACH OTHER!

Maybe you've tried to pray. And maybe the experience feels kind of like attempting to talk on the telephone to a person who's already hung up on you. You're just not making connection. If you've genuinely accepted Jesus as your Savior, it's possible that unconfessed sin is the problem. Or maybe you live in your emotions, instead of living by faith. But it could be that you're trying to talk to someone you've never met!

It is necessary to "examine yourselves to see whether you are in the faith; test yourselves. Do you not realize that Christ Jesus is in you—unless, of course, you fail the test?" (2 Corinthians 13:5).

Does Christ really live in you? What is the test Paul is talking about? Praying "Lord Jesus, come into my heart" isn't a magic formula. Those words need to be accompanied by a daily turning from sin and by surrendering your whole life to God.

If you merely consider Jesus as an "extra boost" to help you work your way to heaven, He is not truly living in you. If your thought life is pure garbage and you don't even feel guilty, Jesus is not being allowed to reside within you. Jesus *is* Lord of the universe, and you can't invite Him to be a prisoner in your inner being—He has to be boss! Either Jesus is Lord of all or He isn't Lord at all.

Do you pass the test? Is Jesus living in you, directing your priorities, choosing your friends, managing your money, enjoying your leisure time, and guiding you in what to say? Or is there an emptiness inside, making God seem like an inhabitant of outer space with whom you communicate only in case of emergency?

If Jesus doesn't really *live* in you, ask yourself some questions: Are you willing to be a private in the army of General Jesus? Are you ready to obey His commandments? (He'll give you the power.) Can you admit that all your good deeds have mixed motives and are so hopelessly self-serving that you're really a pretty terrible sinner? Do you hate your sin enough to really want to change? Are you willing to be considered weird for Jesus—and to follow Him, even if it means losing some friends?

If you can answer yes to every one, you're ready to make a revolutionary commitment to Jesus. As you honestly admit that you were wrong to break God's rules, the blood of Jesus, poured out on the cross, takes away all your sins. By opening the door of your heart, you allow the Spirit of Jesus supernaturally to come live within you.

Your part is praying in faith, with a life totally surrendered to Jesus. He'll invade your being and completely fulfill His promise: "Whoever believes in me, as the Scripture has said, streams of living water will flow from within him" (John 7:38).

The following is a guideline prayer for you to communicate your desire to Jesus, who poured out His own blood on a cross so your sins can be canceled:

> Lord Jesus, I believe that You are the Son of God who rose from the dead and who will come again in power and great glory. I know that I'm a sinner and I've done a lot of things I shouldn't have done. I now hate those things and want to stop doing them. Thank You that You died on the cross, and that Your blood can erase my sin. Please forgive me and give me a clean heart.
>
> I open my life to You, asking You to come in and run my life. I want to obey You. I want You to be Number One in my life. What

Your Bible calls sin I'll avoid; and I will obey Your comandments. I
trust You for the power to do this. I ask You to take control of my life
and make me the person You want me to be. Thank You for coming
into my life as You promised. In Jesus' Name. Amen. (Let it be so!)

Surrendering to Jesus is an exciting new start. Jesus has become
your best Friend, your infallible Guide, your constant Comforter, the
Giver of love, joy, and peace, and the Right Way to go.

The most worthy goal you could ever set for yourself is to get to
know Him better and better.

Chapter Two
"I Just Need to Talk to Somebody"

Rochelle had always loved Christmas. Decorating the tree. Shopping, with all its wonderful surprises. The evening she always helped her mom decorate sugar cookies in the shapes of bells and stars. Caroling with the youth group. And the special time together as a family. Rochelle knew she was a little too taken with presents, turkey dinner, and hoping for new-fallen snow on December 24, but she did remember that divine Baby who came to die for her sins. She thanked God for sending the Savior into a troubled and mixed-up world.

This year started like every other Christmas as a special spirit of joy and anticipation filled the air. Her little sister, Amanda, excitedly told everyone that she was too old for dolls and wanted a chemistry set. Her mom was happily involved in preparing her Sunday school class for their part in the Christmas program, and her dad didn't mind putting in long hours at the drugstore because the extra Christmas sales would pay for their family vacation at the beach.

When Rochelle's brother, Dave, called from college to ask if his roommate could spend Christmas with the family, their dad had assured him that friends were always welcome in their home. No one gave the visitor a second thought—until they picked them up at the airport. As Dave and Jeremy neared the gate, it was easy to see that the clean-cut kid who had left home for college in September had changed a great deal. Dave was unshaven. His sloppy and exotic clothing made him stand out from the crowd. His friend, Jeremy, had long scraggly hair, an earring, and gaudy jewelry. Although there were hugs and greetings, everyone was obviously uncomfortable. Dave seemed more interested in Jeremy than in his own family, whom he hadn't seen for four months. Rochelle's mom tried to ease the tension by announcing there would be stuffed pork chops, mashed potatoes, and lemon pie for dinner—all of Dave's favorites. But Dave seemed unimpressed.

Rochelle helped to get all the food on the table, and then everyone was called to the dining room. The Yuletide centerpiece and lit candles did nothing to replace the gloom. After the blessing, everyone ate in awkward silence.

Finally, Dave spoke up. "There's something I need to tell you. I've discovered that I'm gay. I know this may be hard for you to understand, but I was born that way and all I can do is live out my destiny. Jeremy and I love each other, and I'm asking you to accept me as I am."

Desperately trying to control the anger in his voice, Rochelle's father asked bitterly, "Son, how could you ever do this to me?" Then he got up from the table and grabbed his jacket from the coat closet. He slammed out the door, started the car, and drove away.

Rochelle's mom began to cry—then broke into hysterical sobbing. Amanda's confusion also turned into tears. Rochelle, not knowing what to do, tried to put an arm around both her mother and sister. Dave and Jeremy could only retreat to Dave's room.

When Rochelle's mom and sister quieted down, the three of them just sat there. Stunned. Unmoving. In a while her dad returned and told Amanda that she was spending the night at a cousin's house and that she needed to pack her suitcase quickly.

"Rochelle," he said kindly, "your mom and I are going out for coffee so we can talk. We'll be back before ten o'clock."

Within a few minutes they were gone. Dave emerged and informed Rochelle that he and Jeremy were going for a walk in the moonlight.

So she was left home alone. It had taken only four hours for Rochelle's whole world to cave in.

Sure, she felt bad that Christmas had been ruined—but there were worse things to face. She'd always been close to Dave and had admired him as her older brother. He'd been taught the Bible just as she had, and he knew that the Scriptures state that a homosexual lifestyle is sinful. Dave had dated her best friend, Kathy, for a year and a half, and he'd always seemed interested in girls. What could have changed his mind? What had happened to him?

And how could her parents be so concerned about their own problems that they had completely forgotten about her? Where could she turn? What could she do?

Rochelle felt she couldn't call Kathy, because Kathy still liked Dave and this would break her heart. Sara was a caring person—but she liked to gossip and couldn't be trusted with a situation like this.

Her Bible study leader had said, "Just call me any time if you have a problem." That time was now.

Rochelle called—only to find out from one of her roommates that she had already left to spend the holidays with family.

Although Rochelle felt self-conscious, in desperation she dialed her youth pastor—only to get a recorded message. And then it hit her that her parents may want to keep this a secret. They were always so concerned about the family image. Maybe she'd never be able to talk to *anyone.*

She felt totally alone.

As she walked into the living room, the picture of Jesus above the fireplace mantel caught her eye. She stopped short. It was just as if Jesus were putting words into her mind: *You can talk to me. I won't tell anyone. I'll understand. And most of all, I have all power—so I can really help you. I love you so much, I died for you.*

Why didn't she think of talking to Jesus first?

YOU HAVE AN APPOINTMENT WITH THE CREATOR OF THE UNIVERSE...

...to learn to pray in difficult situations.

You can talk over any problem with God. You don't need any fancy words or set formulas. As you pray, include any Bible verses you remember which relate to the topic. That brings your mind back to God's point of view on the matter. But if you don't know much about the Bible, just pour out your heart to the God who loves you. He'll listen. He'll understand. In His right time He'll answer.

Sometimes, situations in your life can feel so overwhelming that you don't even know how to begin praying. Check out these suggested prayer-starters. They may be just what you need to get you going and keep your heart-needs in their right place—which is in God's hands, not yours!

Praying When the Guy or Girl You Like Rejects You

DAY 1

Dear God, You know I've liked _____ for a long time now, and _____ doesn't feel the same way about me. That really hurts. Sometimes it makes me feel like asking, "What's wrong with me?"

Then I need to remember Your words: "I have loved you with an everlasting love; I have drawn you with loving-kindness. I will build you up again..." (Jeremiah 31:3–4). When others let me down, You're there to encourage me. Even if no one else loves me, You do. Thank You that when I question who I am and my value as a person, You're there to tell me: "Before I formed you in the womb I knew you, before you were born I set you apart" (Jeremiah 1:5). You loved me so much You sent Jesus to die for me, so I know I'm worth a whole lot.

If I compare myself with kids that get more dates than a palm tree I feel inferior. Then I wish I were so good-looking that just my presence would make a statement. It would be nice to be popular.

Then I need to focus on Your standards: "But the Lord said to Samuel, 'Do not consider his appearance or his height, for I have rejected him. The Lord does not look at the things man looks at. Man looks at the outward appearance but the Lord looks at the heart' " (1 Samuel 16:7). "Charm is deceptive, and beauty is fleeting; but a woman who fears the Lord is to be praised" (Proverbs 31:30). Lord, keep reminding me of Your standard of inner attractiveness. I want to be free from worrying about every zit, having to be super-thin, striving for a body that would make it in Hollywood, and having to wear just what everyone else decides is the in thing. That's slavery and I don't want it. Thank You for the design You used in creating me. I know that the person

You've picked out for me to marry will love me just the way I am.

Lord, even though the thing I want most right now is for
_____ to like me, I know You have a plan for my whole life, one
that's better than any I could come up with on my own. You said: " 'For
I know the plans I have for you,' declares the Lord, 'plans to prosper
you and not to harm you, plans to give you hope and a future' "
(Jeremiah 29:11). God, right now, I give up my will in order to find
Yours. If You want me to go out with _____, change his/her
heart. If this isn't part of Your plan for my life I accept that, and I ask
You to heal my emotions. Thank You that You're a surgeon, capable of
such a delicate operation. You're the One who "heals the brokenhearted
and binds up their wounds" (Psalm 147:3).

I will let Your love fill the void left in my heart because
_____ won't reciprocate my feelings. Thank You for the
promise: "And my God will meet all your needs according to his glorious riches in Christ Jesus" (Philippians 4:19). That means I can receive
from You all the love, all the acceptance, and all the companionship
that I need—even if _____ chooses to pay no attention to me
whatever. I just want to tell You, Jesus, that I love You very much and
that You're all I need.

Praying When Your Parents Have Too Many of Their Own Problems to Care About You — DAY 2

Dear God, I'd like to have parents who loved me enough to take
time to listen, who loved me enough to check where I am without
treating me like a baby, and who weren't too busy to take an interest
in things that are important to me. But I know *I* can't change either
my dad or my mom. They have so many of their own issues that
they're incapable of reaching out to me as I want them to. They really
don't understand how much I need them to be there for me.

But, God, You can fill in whenever they blow it. I can say, with the
guy who wrote the Psalms: "Though my father and mother forsake
me, the Lord will receive me" (Psalm 27:10). You are the Father to the
fatherless, the Dad who will never let me down.

It's so hard when my best isn't good enough. I don't know what my
mom/dad really expects. I can't be like _____ and I'm not good

at_____. It hurts me so much when he/she says, "_____

_____
_____ ."

I thank You that You always act the way a father is supposed to act. "As a father has compassion on his children, so the Lord has compassion on those who fear him; for he knows how we are formed, he remembers that we are dust" (Psalm 103:13–14). When I feel distressed because I can't measure up to the standards my parents have set for me, I'll escape into Your arms, knowing that You love me without any conditions. "But God demonstrates his own love for us in this: While we were still sinners, Christ died for us" (Romans 5:8). In fact, You would have sent Jesus to die for me even if I had never accepted Him as my Savior—and that proves Your love isn't based on my performance. Thanks for loving me just the way I am.

Lord, help me to forgive my parents. I know Your Bible says: "Be kind and compassionate to one another, forgiving each other, just as in Christ God forgave you" (Ephesians 4:32). That includes parents. I know You never give any orders without providing the power supply necessary for the task. I understand that I forgive with my will—not with my emotions. I forgive my mom for _____ and _____
and I forgive my dad for _____ and _____ .

My emotions may still go wild, but that's okay. Sooner or later they will catch up with my will. Each time my parents are unfair, each time they hurt me, and every time they fail me, I will plug into Your love-your-enemies love and receive the power to forgive them.

Lord, give me some good ideas on how to serve them and meet their needs. Show me something special I can do for my mom today, to make her day more pleasant. How can I demonstrate to my father that I love him? Thank You, God, for my parents. I know You had a special reason for giving them to me, and I'm grateful.

Praying When You Have That Stop-the-World-I-Want-To-Get-Off Feeling

DAY
3

Lord, today I really feel depressed. Nothing seems to be going right and I don't really think I'm very important to anybody. Because of _____and,

_____

this week has been terrible. The thought that the world would be better off without me and I might just as well end it all has crossed my mind. However, I recognize that idea as being from the devil. Jesus, I remember that You said, "The thief" [and that's the devil] "comes only to steal and kill and destroy; I have come that they may have life, and have it to the full" (John 10:10). I can see that the enemy is trying to implement his killer strategy by getting me to take my own life, and I won't buy it.

Your Word also points out: "Be self-controlled and alert. Your enemy the devil prowls around like a roaring lion looking for someone to devour. Resist him, standing firm in the faith" (1 Peter 5:8–9). The worst thing I can do is just accept all these crazy thoughts as being my own.

Instead, I'll take my stand on James 4:7: "Submit yourselves, then, to God. Resist the devil, and he will flee from you." This means that instead of focusing my eyes on the present problems, I'll turn my mind toward the One who lives in me and "is greater than the one who is in the world" (1 John 4:4).

God, instead of looking at my circumstances which right now are a real bummer, I choose to look at the long-term picture and believe what You say about me. You created me with a purpose and You tell me the same thing You told Jeremiah: "Before I formed you in the womb I knew you, before you were born I set you apart" (Jeremiah 1:5). And then You give me the great promise that You "will fulfill your purpose for me" (Psalm 138:8 *personalized*). I think You wrote Hebrews 10:35–36 especially for me because You knew someday I'd feel this way: "So do not throw away your confidence; it will be richly rewarded. You need to persevere so that when you have done the will of God, you will receive what he has promised."

Lord, I want to stick with You and keep the faith, but I have to get through this day. Like David, I'll ask myself a question: "Why are you downcast, O my soul? Why so disturbed within me?" (Psalm 42:5).

God, the reason I'm so discouraged is because _____

_____

and_____.

Plus, school is so boring, things at home are tense, and_____

But, Lord, I do have to admit that no one ever died of boredom and You're such a powerful God You can change each of these things. My problem is that I'm looking at today *only* and not viewing my whole life in perspective. I remember that some time ago _____ seemed like such a terrible problem, and now I hardly think of it. Right now I can't forget that You can either make me so strong I can withstand the pressure or You can remove the situation. I'll trust You.

Lord, I guess I'm on my way out to face Goliath. I admit that I like Your miracles—but only after they're over! I really don't enjoy the situations that lead up to them. For the present, God, help me to concentrate on believing that You said, "Those who hope in me will not be disappointed" (Isaiah 49:23). Lord, I do put my trust in You and believe what Your Word says: "Yet the Lord longs to be gracious to you; he rises to show you compassion, For the Lord is a God of justice. *Blessed are all who wait for him!*" (Isaiah 30:18, italics mine). Actually, Lord, You put it in even stronger terms: "Be still before the Lord and wait patiently for him" (Psalm 37:7)—a command that's hard for me to obey! Instead of doing anything drastic, help me to do the hardest thing in the world for me—to wait until You deal with the impossible circumstances.

Thank You that there is hope. Like David, I'm telling myself: "Find rest, O my soul, in God alone; my hope comes from him" (Psalm 62:5).

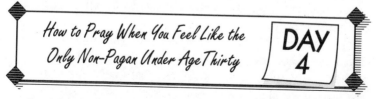

How to Pray When You Feel Like the Only Non-Pagan Under Age Thirty — DAY 4

Lord, to be perfectly honest, I'm tired of being good! Almost everybody else cheats on tests. I get so much static about being a virgin—actually you'd think it was a crime or something. I could dress as nice as the other kids—if only I did a little shoplifting. I can never say I've seen the ultimate sex-and-violence movie. I know I shouldn't fill my mind with such garbage, but I'm tired of being out of it. My life is pretty boring and I wonder what it would be like to get high, or to win a lot of money gambling, or to _____

_____.

But then I remember something inspiring: "By faith Moses, when he had grown up, refused to be known as the son of pharaoh's daughter. He chose to be mistreated along with the people of God rather than to enjoy the pleasure of sin for a short time. He regarded disgrace for the sake of Christ as of greater value than the treasure of Egypt, because he was looking ahead to his reward" (Hebrews 11:24–26). And he got his prize—not only in heaven but on earth. How exciting it must have been to experience God's miracles—the plagues, the Red Sea opening, manna from heaven, water from a rock! How exhilarating to be so close to God and so at home in His presence—to see His glory and receive the Ten Commandments. But, Lord, I know that Moses could have thrown it all away for one "secret affair" with an Egyptian princess, a fascination with wealth or power, or running around with royal renegades. Right now I need to concentrate on his example, and hang in there!

Whenever I start feeling like I can't swim against the current any longer, I need to realize that it's because I've stopped depending on You for my joy, my companionship, my fun, my friends, my love for life—everything. I've sluffed off on spending time with You, so I've absorbed a media mentality instead of Your hatred for sin. I've let so many trivial distractions blur my awe for Your command: "Be holy, because I am holy" (1 Peter 1:16). It's been a while since I've sensed Your presence so keenly that I just wanted to stay with You and nothing else really mattered. I know that the solution to my lackluster living is getting alone with You, expecting to receive Your answers.

I forget that Philippians 4:19 is really true: "And my God will meet all your needs according to his glorious riches in Christ Jesus." Instead of muddling through, I *can* ask You for what I need. Lord, put some new spark in my life. Show me how to practice 1 Peter 3:13–14: "Who is going to harm you if you are eager to do good? But even if you should suffer for what is right, you are blessed. Do not fear what they fear; do not be frightened." I claim Isaiah 64:5: "You come to the help of those who gladly do right, who remember your ways." Make me so enthusiastic about doing what is right that I set the pace, instead of falling in line with the rest. Use me to make doing good so contagious that other kids become curious and even jealous! Put me in contact with some other young people all pumped up to serve You. Lord, I ask You for

and_____.

Give me a new hunger for Your Word. I take Psalm 119:1–3 literally: "Blessed are they whose ways are blameless, who walk according to the law of the Lord. Blessed are they who keep his statutes and seek him with all their heart. They do nothing wrong; they walk in his ways." I want to be that kind of person.

I would like to memorize enough Bible verses so I can say with David, "I have hidden your word in my heart that I might not sin against you" (Psalm 119:11). I want to be able to repeat Psalm 119:15–16 and mean it: "I meditate on your precepts and consider your ways, I delight in your decrees; I will not neglect your word." I realize that if I swallow the secular humanism I get all day at school, and choose to listen to media-ized morality, then I won't have much incentive for righteous living. Your Word poses a question and then answers it: "How can a young [person] keep his way pure? By living according to your word" (Psalm 119:9).

If my mind isn't continually cleansed by my applying Your words, I'll lose strength and just float downstream with everyone else. I guess I better stop complaining and open my Bible! Thanks for listening.

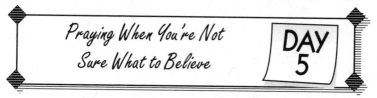

Praying When You're Not Sure What to Believe

DAY 5

Dear God, if I'm totally honest, I have to admit to You that I have doubts about the Bible and what I've been taught as a Christian. I keep hearing that "safe sex" is okay if I'm old enough to handle it and if I really love the other person. I hear that abortion is only the removal of some unwanted tissue, that practicing homosexuality is perfectly fine, that lying is okay in certain circumstances, that evolution accounts for life on this planet, and that no one believes the "fairy tale" about Adam and Eve and the snake. I feel kind of weird for having different opinions than everyone else about almost everything. After hearing the same thing over and over, I start to think it's true. I'm confused. Please help me.

One thing that really gives me hope is the way You treated Thomas when he said, "Unless I see the nail marks in his hands and put my finger where the nails were, and put my hand into his side, I will not believe it" (John 20:25). You didn't bawl him out or tell him he was terrible. You said, "Put your finger here; see my hands. Reach out

your hand and put it into my side. Stop doubting and believe" (John 20:27). Thank You that You welcome honest doubters.

When Thomas saw the evidence, he exclaimed, "My Lord and my God!" Right now, Lord, I remember a speaker who said this: "Most doubts aren't intellectual—they're moral. The gal who's sleeping with her boyfriend starts having doubts about the Bible being the Word of God because she enjoys what she's doing and doesn't want to believe it's sin. If we believe we got here by chance, we're responsible to no one—but if a loving and all-powerful God created us, we're accountable to Him. A person who has aspirations of being his or her own god can't possibly accept being fashioned by a God who has His own plan for us. Those who believe that the opinion of the majority sets the standard of right and wrong consider man, not God, the ultimate authority!" So I guess it's important to find the source of my doubts. That's kind of scary. I guess I better check my own life first.

Lord, do I question Your Word because there's a sin I don't want to give up? I admit _____

and _____
are things I'd rather not consider wrong, even though the Bible says
they are. God, if I'm going to be honest, I must consider the possibility of my own ungodly desires playing a part in my doubts. (*STOP and
LISTEN*, so God can speak to you. Write out your personal prayer to
Him:) _____

_____
_____
_____ .

   Lord, I feel like the father of the tormented boy who cried, "I do
believe; help me overcome my unbelief" (Mark 9:24). God, show me
the way out of the doubts I have. I give You any habit, addiction, desire,
or thought pattern that would keep me from believing what You have
to say. I think _____
may be interfering with my faith. (IF YOU'RE NOT READY TO PRAY
THIS, DON'T.) I surrender that part of my life to You.
   However, _____
and _____
still bother me. Lord, I pray that You'll show me who I can talk to in
order to get my honest questions answered. Is there a book I should
read? If so, lead me to it.
   God, in some ways, I may be making this a little too complicated.
Hebrews 11:6 gets to the heart of the matter: "And without faith it is
impossible to please God, because anyone who comes to him must
believe that he exists and that he rewards those who earnestly seek
him." I do believe You're there. I choose to put my faith in the fact that
You'll reward those who choose to follow You. And I can't really go
after You without searching the Scriptures. That gets back to "faith
comes from hearing the message, and the message is heard through
the word of Christ" (Romans 10:17). I have to admit that I get a lot
more input from the other side than I do from Your Book. When I read
it from the Bible, You seem perfectly capable of creating the world—
it's only in _____ class that I have doubts. Your Ten
Commandments read from Exodus 20 seem perfectly reasonable—it's
only when _____
happens that I wonder.
   I'm probably hanging out too much with some of the wrong people. I can't really say with David, "As for the saints who are in the land,
they are the glorious ones in whom is all my delight" (Psalm 16:3).

More Christian friends would really help. Lord, I'm willing to give up my friendship with _____ and _____. (DON'T FILL IN THE BLANKS IF YOU DON'T MEAN IT!) God, please bring the right people into my life.

God, I guess I shouldn't expect that being Your follower will be easy. I'm willing to engage in whatever spiritual warfare is necessary to be able to say at the end of my life, "I have fought the good fight, I have finished the race, I have kept the faith" (2 Timothy 4:7).

Chapter Three
Before the Roof Caves In

Although the countless lights he was staring at indicated the presence of plenty of people, Jeff felt totally alone. The spectacular view of New York City by night framed by the picture window his parents loved so much only made his world more dark and depressing. He just couldn't shake the feeling of emptiness and despair. He'd give anything just to move back to their small town in Georgia.

It just didn't seem fair. Why couldn't his father see that the happiness of his family was more important than a big promotion and a huge salary increase?

Was he really the guy who had led his team to victory in Bible quizzing competition? Was he the same kid who had taught the most successful Bible study group sponsored by the student ministry on his campus? Could he really be the junior who had led more kids to Christ than anyone else in Everyday Evangelism—who had been elected president of his church youth group, and who fearlessly stood for Christian values in his classes?

But that was the former Jeff Thompson. The Jeff of today felt more like a mission field, not a missionary. There was no Bible club, no Christians to hang around with—not even someone who appeared to be less pagan than the rest. He was the weird kid with the southern accent who was constantly out of step. He hadn't even tried to witness to anyone—probably because he wasn't quite sure he had any faith to share. Because of his father's workload, they'd only visited a couple churches, both of which seemed cold and impersonal. The roof was caving in, and Jeff couldn't find any strength to prop it up.

He really couldn't put his finger on the problem. He hadn't decided to become an atheist, to do drugs, or to run away from home. He didn't even think he was mad at God—confused and a little bitter maybe, but much too empty to express any strong emotions. He was still going through the motions of being "good," but no matter what he did, none of the old enthusiasm returned. God seemed so far away that Jeff wasn't even sure they were on speaking terms. What had gone wrong...?

You may not be able to identify with Jeff and his early success. Perhaps you're a *struggling-to-keep-your-head-above-water* Christian. Maybe you've thought that if you could do the things Jeff did, you'd never have any more doubts or feel like throwing in the towel. You might be relieved to learn that the supports which keep the more visible aspects of your Christian life in place can be erected by anyone—not just the talented and personable Jeffs of this world. Keep reading....

Jeff, like so many Christians young and old, had neglected a very important part of his spiritual life—time alone with God, reading His Word, meditating on Scripture, listening for His instructions, and praying. His Christianity was based entirely on external events—attending a good church, witnessing, Bible study for the purpose of gathering information or presenting a lesson to others, and working with organized Christians. These things are very good and form part of a well-balanced Christian life, but they will all cave in unless they can be supported by a strong framework underneath—a personal communication with God. Once Jeff didn't have his church, his youth group, and his school Bible club, he was lost. He didn't know how to approach God as an individual.

The super-structure of "serving God," "being active in church," or "maintaining a good testimony" must be held up by the pillars of personal intimacy with God.

George Muller was a man who, for sixty-two years, prayed in all the funds he needed to support thousands of orphans without ever once asking any individual for money. He describes his private time with God as an exciting adventure. He never knew how God would supply his needs but he trusted Him completely. Prayer was his source of peace and relaxation. When his only daughter was gravely ill, he could totally rest in God. His life was a continuous and enjoyable conversation with his Best Friend! But if he had never learned to pray, no one today would have ever heard of George Muller.

There are many very ordinary people who know how to pray, how to practice the presence of God, and how to live in His peace. Because of that, whatever else they do in life—whether it is teaching a Bible study, working in an office, baking a cake, cheering a discouraged person, or taking a test, it is done with a love and excellence which shows that they have been with Jesus.

If someone like Jeff could really be convinced that time alone with God each day is a top priority, the fight he'd have on his hands might go something like this...

As he stared out into the night, Jeff remembered the words of his youth pastor back in Georgia: "If you don't have a daily quiet time in which you really meet God, you'll probably be able to win a few short races—but you'll have to drop out of the marathon. The spiritual resources to keep going when things get really tough come from reading your Bible and praying each day." At the time, Jeff had paid little attention, because he thought he'd discovered a shortcut to spiritual success. *Wow,* thought Jeff, *this must be exactly the situation Pastor Phil was talking about. I might as well give it a try.*

He set his alarm to ring fifteen minutes early, then fell asleep.

But because he'd stayed up late, he automatically turned the alarm off and plopped his head back down onto the pillow. The next thing he knew his mom was informing him that he'd overslept. That evening he decided to try again. He thought he'd finish his homework early and then snatch fifteen minutes in his room, but he just couldn't tear himself away from the basketball game on TV. Later, he tried to pray before going to bed, but immediately zonked out.

Finally, four days later, he succeeded in getting up when his alarm rang and went to the bathroom to splash cold water on his face so he'd stay awake. He hadn't really studied enough for his Spanish test, however, and kept interrupting Genesis 1 and 2 in order to peek at the vocabulary words he should have memorized. Of course everybody sleeps in on Saturday, and Jeff did too. When he awoke, he was starved. After three bowls of cereal, he thought he'd return to his room to read the Bible. But when his sister wanted to play tennis, he felt embarrassed telling her he wanted to have devotions first.

Deciding that reading the whole Bible through was a little too ambitious, he began the New Testament. When he got bogged down with the genealogy of Matthew 1, he convinced himself that since he wasn't getting anything out of it he might as well read the comics—and he did. A couple days later, he opted for praying rather than Bible reading. He prayed about everything he could think of, and then checked his watch. He'd prayed for three minutes and forty-nine seconds!

Jeff couldn't believe how hard it was to establish a quiet time—to say nothing about honestly and effectively communicating with God. Did all those super-Christians start out like this? Was it worth trying to hang in there? He certainly hadn't noticed any dramatic change in his life.

The next day, he got a terrible sore throat and was in bed for two days. He never even thought of reading his Bible. The third day, he felt a lot better and opened his Bible to Matthew 4. As he read, "Man does not live on bread alone, but on every word that comes from the mouth of God," he saw something new. He *needed* God's words to live by just as much as he needed meat and potatoes and vegetables. He could only receive spiritual nourishment if he kept on reading his Bible. In the physical realm we don't always remember what we eat but it keeps us healthy. *Maybe reading the Bible is like that,* Jeff reasoned. *Maybe the chapter I read a week ago and don't remember now is still giving me spiritual energy.* This idea gave him the incentive to persevere....

This won't be the end of Jeff's struggles. If he keeps at it for a year, he'll probably have the habit of daily devotions pretty well established. However, the devil will work just as hard to break the habit as he did to prevent it in the first place. A daily quiet time will never be easy—but it will always be worth every bit of struggle it takes!

📝 Don't Just Sit There—Do Something!

Start tomorrow by scheduling ten minutes into your day for Bible reading and prayer.

1. *Establish a time.*
   a. Begin with a ten-minute time slot (maybe even five or seven minutes), and once you've firmly established this habit, gradually increase the time spent. Biting off too big a chunk will be programming yourself for failure.
   b. Stick with the same time every day, so you'll form a habit.
   c. Give God the best ten minutes of your day. Early in the morning is usually the quietest time and the most free of interruptions. However, a night person might be more successful placing an appointment with God just before going to bed. If both your parents work and you come home to an empty house, you may want to schedule your quiet time when you get home from school.

2. *Choose a quiet place where you can be alone.*
   a. If you don't have your own room, you may have to use some creativity—the basement, the park, the hallway of your apartment building, and even the bathroom are possibilities.
   b. Buy some earplugs if you need to!

3. *Develop an attitude of perseverance.* Don't become discouraged even if:

    a. You miss several days in a row.

    b. You lose your Bible.

    c. Some days you find it nearly impossible to pray.

    d. You have trouble concentrating and feel you don't get much out of your reading.

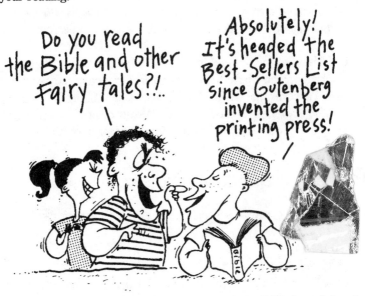

    e. Somebody in your family thinks reading the Bible is weird and delights in persecuting you.

    f. You find some passages hard to understand.

    g. You're a "noise addict," who goes nuts without a TV or radio in the background and have to kick the media habit cold turkey in order to establish a quiet time. (It is possible to listen to quiet praise music during your devotions.)

4. *Establish a system of accountability.*

    a. Decide to report to someone each week, telling him/her whether or not you spent time with God every day. This person could be a friend and you could become mutually accountable to each other. Or you could ask a parent, pastor, or youth worker to check up on you each week.

    b. Keep some kind of chart for yourself. The easiest is to use a calendar, checking off the day after having your quiet time.

Just in case you wondered, almost everybody starts out like Jeff did. The devil will fight you every inch of the way if you decide to saturate your life with Scripture and really learn to pray. That's because you're about to discover more and more secrets to victorious Christian living. At age eighty-five, you still won't be bored because you'll continue to learn new things about our wonderful God.

And this exciting adventure will begin only when you start by giving God just ten minutes a day!

YOU HAVE AN APPOINTMENT WITH THE CREATOR OF THE UNIVERSE...
...to learn to pray the Bible.

Make an "Appointment With God" calendar like the one on the next page. On Sunday, choose the time you'll meet God each day and then check whether or not you kept the appointment. If something unexpected changes your schedule and you spend your ten minutes with God at another time, congratulations. You should count it as an appointment you kept.

Praying the Scriptures is one very effective way of using ten minutes with God. This was the system used by George Muller, whose life and ministry have affected millions. He began his devotions by reading a passage of Scripture, and as a certain Bible verse reminded him to pray for something, he stopped reading and lifted up the petition to God and then continued reading until another verse prompted him to pray for something else.

"Praying Through the Book of James" is meant to teach you Scripture praying, so you can use it in your quiet time. *After going through the first couple of chapters, reading the verses indicated and then praying the written prayer, read chapters three, four, and five on your own, praying the things God brings to your mind before using the format found in this book.* Then go on to pray through some other epistles of the New Testament.

Appointment Calendar

Sunday	Monday	Tuesday	Wednesday	Thursday	Friday	Saturday
☐ Talk to God from: ____ to: ____	☐ Talk to God from: ____ to: ____	☐ Talk to God from: ____ to: ____	☐ Talk to God from: ____ to: ____	☐ Talk to God from: ____ to: ____	☐ Talk to God from: ____ to: ____	☐ Talk to God from: ____ to: ____

Check off appointments you kept.

Praying Through James, Chapter One   **DAY 1**

Read verse 1

Lord, James considered himself Your humble servant, but I sometimes act as if I were Your boss! Forgive me for my arrogance. Give me the heart of a servant, a willingness to always follow Your directions. Sometimes what You ask of me isn't what I enjoy doing._____

_____

and _____

are things I know would please You but I find them difficult. Help me to be the kind of servant who instantly obeys without counting the cost.

Read verses 2-4

I must confess that I haven't faced my present trial, which is _____

_____,

with joy. Lord, I ask You to replace my bad attitudes with godly ones. Thank You that this problem will teach me patience and perseverance if I keep my eyes fixed on You through it all.

Read verses 5-8

_____

is a big dilemma for me right now. In faith, I ask You for wisdom and I wait to receive it. I'll do my part by studying all Your Word has to say on the topic, asking the advice of a mature Christian, and praying each day for wisdom. Thank You that I can stop worrying about it and trust You to supply the wisdom I need.

Read verses 9-11

Keep me from being so materialistic. Give me Your sense of values. I rejoice that I'm a child of the King, with a mansion reserved in heaven. The Creator of the universe takes special care of me. And I have access to the power that raised Jesus Christ from the dead. Forgive me for being so taken up with trivial toys and trinkets. I realize that my new _____, the _____ I like so much, and everything else I can accumulate on earth will one day be worthless. I and the poorest person on earth are equal before You. I've been so anxious to buy _____ that I've nearly forgotten to put You first. I'm sorry and I want to change.

Read verses 12-15

Thank You, God, that You give prizes to those who take Your tests and pass. _____ is a big temptation right now. I realize I can never use the excuse, "It's God's fault for letting me get into this situation." It isn't. If I didn't have wrong desires I wouldn't even be tempted. Lord, I surrender my bad motives to You, and ask You for victory.

Read verses 16-18

Thank You for _____, _____, and _____, which are good gifts You've given me. Thank You that You're a never-changing God, whom I can count on to continue giving me what is good. Thank You that I heard Your Word, so that I could be saved.

Read verses 19-21

Lord, forgive me for having such a short fuse and getting angry at _____. Help me to be slower to speak my mind. Lord, I want Your Word to be planted and to grow in me so that it brings forth fruit in my actions.

Read verses 22-25

Lord, so often I just hear Your Word and never put it into practice. Then it really does me no good. A truth from James, chapter one, which I know You want me to put into practice, is _____
_____

Lord, I will do it. (DON'T PRAY THIS UNLESS YOU MEAN IT!)

Read verses 26-27

Lord, help me to be more careful about the words that come out of my lips! Keep me from being so busy with the things that concern me that I don't have time to help people less fortunate than I. Right now You're convicting me to spend time helping _____. Draw me closer and closer to You so I don't get caught in the muck of the world.

Praying Through James, Chapter Two **DAY 2**

Read verses 1-12

Lord, the biggest divisions used to be between the rich and the poor—but at my school it's between the cool and the uncool! I have to admit I don't want to commit social suicide by being a friend to _____. And at our youth group, things aren't much different. We don't welcome _____ into our clique. And if I hang around with him/her, the other kids will probably ignore me. I've been as guilty as the rest of giving _____ the cold shoulder.

The words "If you show favoritism, you sin" make me a terrible sinner. I confess my wrongdoing to You and ask Your help in one of the hardest things You've ever asked of me—giving up my popularity to spend time with _____. (DON'T FILL IN THE BLANK IF YOU DON'T MEAN IT.)

I know that when I really obey You, I always experience freedom, because my conscience becomes clear. Give me Your power, because I sure can't handle this one on my own. Yet, I know that if I can't show compassion to _____, I can't expect to receive Your mercy.

Read verses 14-26

I realize that all I say about loving You and having faith in You mean nothing unless I walk my talk. What I am speaks so loudly that no

one really hears my words. I declare that I love Jesus more than any-one, but I spend all my time thinking about_____
_____.

I say my first priority is serving You, but if I'm perfectly honest, I'd rather not go to Bible study if _____
is on TV. I express concern for the poor people of the third world, but instead of giving my money in the offering to help them, I use it to buy _____, which I really don't need anyway.

Lord, keep me from being a hypocrite—saying that I believe You'll take care of me, but being a practicing atheist who carries the world on my shoulders by worrying every step of the way. I'd like to obey You like Abraham did—even if You ask me to do something hard.

God, I know I can't work for my salvation—it's all by faith. But if my faith is real, it will show up in my actions.

Praying Through James, Chapter Three **DAY 3**

Read verses 1-12

Lord, I guess I've never thought about how powerful my tongue really is! It can start a false story that will hurt and possibly destroy the reputations of many people. It can lash out in anger and criticism, inflicting deep emotional wounds. It can tell a lie, which can cause untold trouble. It can make fun of the kid who is already contemplating suicide. My tongue and I plead guilty to _____
_____.

But my tongue can also give my mother an honest compliment, which will make her day. It can express love and caring, which will lift the spirits of a lonely or discouraged person. It can explain the truth of the gospel and lead another person to saving faith. It can praise and thank God. It can express faith and confidence in God, encouraging and motivating those around me.

Lord, I give You my tongue. I find it easier to sin with words than with actions. Going from praising You to criticizing Your other children all in one breath can happen before I know it. I must constantly depend on Your power, or I'll never make it.

Read verses 13-18

Lord, I need Your wisdom. It'll cause me to do the right thing with a humble spirit. Keep me from being envious of _____ and from the selfishness that often makes me want to _____

_____.

Lord, when I think I'm right and want to push others around, I don't have Your wisdom. When I decide the end justifies the means and I can step on a few toes to get the job done, I don't have Your wisdom. When I play favorites and am not completely honest with everyone, I don't have Your wisdom.

Give me the wisdom that imitates You in every situation.

Praying Through James, Chapter Four DAY 4

Read verses 1-3

Forgive me, Lord, for striving and sometimes quarreling with others to try to get what I want. I realize that You're the One who will give me everything if I only bring my petitions before You. But when I ask You for things, I'll remember that You know more than I do, and that Your will is more important than mine.

Read verses 4-5

I also realize that what's on TV, what I usually hear around school, and the conversations at work are usually opposite to Your ideals and standards. Help me to put so much of Your Word in my mind and stay so close to You that I don't swallow the lies dished out by our society or try to fit in with the world.

Read verses 6-12

Lord, pride is raising its ugly head again and making me think

_____.

In humility I will give myself to You. Thank You that I can resist the devil with his temptation to _____
and I know that he has no choice but to beat it.

Lord, I come near to You, confessing my sin of _____. I ask

50

You to forgive me for being wishy-washy about _____. Instead of trying to be the big cheese, I'll humble myself before You and let You lift me up.

Lord, You're both Father and Judge over me and all my brothers and sisters in Christ. Forgive me for being critical of _____ and passing judgment on _____. From now on, I determine to let You be the Judge.

Read verses 13-16

I have a lot of big plans for the future, and I sometimes forget that unless You give me the next breath, I can't do any of the things I'm dreaming about. Help me to add "If it's God's will" to all schemes for tomorrow.

Keep me from bragging about _____

_____.

Help me remember that if I do something worthwhile it's because You gave the strength and the ability to accomplish it. When I realize that sin includes the good I've left undone as well as committing wrong, I don't have anything to boast about.

Praying Through James, Chapter Five **DAY 5**

Read verses 1-6

Lord, don't let me ever be guilty of making money by taking advantage of someone else. Keep me from ever exaggerating in a sales pitch, trying to sell something without being honest about its defects, or paying someone less than standard wages. I know it's not Your will that I live in luxury and self-indulgence, while some of Your other children are in great need. Lord, show me how to use my money and my resources. How much do You want me to give in the offering this Sunday?

Read verses 7-12

Lord, it would be exciting if You came back just this minute, so I wouldn't have to face _____ and _____. But You've asked me to live here on earth and to be patient with other people, patient in suffering, and patient in keeping Your Word—even when nobody else does. But, Lord, I find myself grumbling against _____. Please forgive me. I'll trust You to work all things together for good.

Read verses 13-18

Lord, teach me to share every part of my life with You. In times of joy my prayer will be filled with prayers of praise. In sickness and trouble my prayers of petition will be shared with others. And, Lord, I know that You will hear and answer. If I've fallen into sin, my prayer will be an honest admission of guilt. I will also admit my faults to others so they can pray for me. Right now my prayer to You is_____

_____.

Thank You for the power of prayer. I want to follow You completely so I can be that righteous person who fulfills the conditions of effective prayer. If Elijah could turn the rain faucets of heaven off and on by his prayers, I certainly can pray for_____

_____.

Read verses 19-20

Lord, I want to be instrumental in bringing those who get spiritually off track back to You. Give me Your wisdom, so I can present Your truth to others.

Chapter Four
Are Your Actions Making You a Stranger to the One Who Loves You Most?

Nathan Smith had fine Christian parents. They loved him, spent time with him and his sister, and provided them with everything they needed. As a kid he considered his family tops and obeyed rules without question. He enjoyed a close relationship with his parents. But as he entered his teen years and realized how strict and old-fashioned his parents appeared to his friends, he began to long for the freedom to try new things. Because he'd always attended Northwest Christian Academy and all social activities centered around church and school, he felt he knew nothing about the "real world."

An unusually talented athlete, Nathan begged for an opportunity to participate in the summer team sports program sponsored by the park board. Warning him about hanging around with the wrong crowd, his parents permitted him to sign up for the baseball team. They required that he give them a schedule of all practices and made him promise to be home a half hour after each game was over.

By far the best pitcher on the team, Nathan became popular immediately. Although these guys swore and talked about things that shocked Nathan, they were nice enough. He couldn't believe how much liberty their parents gave them. The team always went out together after each game. Nathan politely declined a couple of times, but then the team got on his case.

"What's with you, Nathan?" questioned Eric. "Don't you like us or something?"

"Maybe you think you're too good for us," suggested Tim.

"It's not that," Nathan protested. "It's just that..." But he really didn't know how to finish the sentence. Right at that moment his parents were an embarrassment to him.

"Is it that your girl friend is jealous and makes you check in every ten minutes?" Alex suggested.

"Come on," Tyler kidded him. "Why not meet us at Burger King tomorrow night at 10:30? Afterwards, we want you to come out to the park for a drink with us."

Nathan felt every eye was on him. And in that moment an idea occurred. After reporting in with his folks, he could take the screen off his bedroom window and slip out. Since his parents watched the evening news religiously, he could easily drive out the back alley without being noticed.

Friday night, he pitched a two-hitter, got on base three times, and pulled off a home run with a man on second, leading the team to victory over their arch rivals. Amid the celebrating Nathan heard, "We're taking you to Burger King. All you can eat—on us."

"Thanks!" Nathan laughed. "I'll have to stop off at home first. Then I'll meet you there."

Nathan walked into the house and told his parents all about the game. When they turned on the news, he innocently went into his room and closed the door. His conscience was shouting at him as he quietly sneaked out the window, slipped into the car, and drove away. *Free at last.* Or at least that's what he thought at the time.

Nathan enjoyed being the center of attention at their victory party. He hadn't planned to go to the park, but he didn't want to appear weird so he tagged along. And he didn't really drink the can of beer thrust into his hands. He just took a couple of sips.

After a couple of weeks Nathan had perfected his out-the-window escape technique. He did have to tell some lies in order to make his getaway—especially after the times when his family came to see him play. He also had to start drinking in order to be one of the guys.

Although he felt very guilty, there was a strange attraction drawing him toward his new friends and a new lifestyle. There was something comfortable about fitting in and going along with the crowd. And the more he got by with, the bolder he became in his deceit. He left one Saturday night "for youth group," but sneaked out with the guys instead. One time when he was facing a big test he hadn't taken time to study for, his new friends taught him how to hide a cheat-sheet. Nathan was nervous—but when he realized that his teachers assumed a Christian would never cheat, he basically got away with murder.

But something was happening to Nathan inside. He felt like a stranger at home, at school, and at church. Although his conscience was becoming hard, it was awkward to be around his parents. He didn't confide in them as he used to. Secretly finding fault with everything they did, he preferred going to his room and closing the door. Not wanting his folks to catch on, he outwardly obeyed their every request, but his heart just wasn't in it anymore. When his mother ended her usual bits of advice with, "Nathan, I know you'll do the right thing," he felt like telling her the whole story, asking for forgiveness, and starting all over again. But he didn't.

He had always been the kid who hung around after school, making his teachers into his friends. Now he left the minute the bell rang and was sure they were all out to get him. One day Miss Simpson looked at him kindly and said, "Nathan, I can tell something's bothering you. Would you care to share it?" Nathan almost started to cry, but he quickly gained control of his *I-know-what-I'm-doing-and-I-don't-need-any-advice-from-anyone* attitude and walked out of the room.

Nathan's experience can teach us something about establishing a meaningful relationship with God. As the great missionary teacher Andrew Murray once said, "Obedience is the greatest factor in being a friend of God." We can't do our own thing, treat His commandments casually, refuse to let the light of His holiness penetrate certain areas of our lives and *still* expect to enjoy His fellowship. Any time you attempt to explain away a scriptural command or rationalize behavior that deep down inside you know is wrong, you'll find that trying to spend time with God is a drag.

You worship Him not only on your knees but by doing your homework well, by accepting the blame when the mistake was your fault, by comforting the little girl who lost her dog, or by returning the excess change to the department store clerk. A life that says "I love You, Lord" is more important than words.

Jesus didn't say "If you love me, buy a Christian bumper sticker." He didn't advise, "Demonstrate your affection for me by participating in the following church activities...." He simply states: "If anyone loves me, he will obey my teaching. My Father will love him, and we will come to him and make our home with him" (John 14:23). A deep intimate relationship with God is totally dependent on our willingness to obey Him in everything.

When you're in the middle of a fight with God about respecting your parents' wishes, dating a non-Christian, or being nice to Bryan with the big mouth, you can't sense the sweetness of His fellowship. When you're alone with God, the job you left undone, your unwillingness to forgive your friend, or the way you argued with your mother will come back to haunt you. You really have no choice but to make things right with others so there's nothing between you and God.

I remember sitting down one morning to pray before I went to work. I closed my eyes and the "vision" before me was a sink full of dirty dishes—the ones I'd promised my roommates I'd wash. As I walked to the kitchen I realized that soap suds and a Scotch-Brite scouring pad were to be my prelude to prayer! Unless your "quiet time" is just a ritual, you'll find it can be interrupted by remembering all kinds of little disobediences and *less-than-loving* attitudes.

The closeness of God's friendship is so wonderful that any necessary adjustments in your lifestyle are well worth the effort. Usually it's not our inability to concentrate or lack of a good system of Bible study that makes it impossible for us to realize God's presence—it's the kind of lives we live. Isaiah 59:1–2 will always hold true: "Surely the arm of the Lord is not too short to save, nor his ear too dull to hear. But your iniquities have separated you from your God; your sins have hidden his face from you, so that he will not hear." If you want to really get to know God so much that you're willing to pay the price of obedience, you'll surely find Him. You'll discover that the power of the Holy Spirit makes obeying possible. "The just shall live by faith," the faith that God can give them victory over sin. Don't permit your sinful actions to make you a stranger to Jesus—the One who loves you the most.

58

YOU HAVE AN APPOINTMENT WITH THE CREATOR OF THE UNIVERSE...

...to get your life in praying order.

A meaningful devotional life and a close friendship with God can never coexist with disobedience to His revealed will.

In the following Scripture passages, you can discover God's standard for you in certain areas of life. Ask God to change your actions, attitudes, and future plans to fit into the mold He has for your life. Every day, ask Him for the power to live differently and by faith release Him to live His life through you.

Relationships With the Opposite Sex DAY 1

It is God's will that you should be sanctified: that you should avoid sexual immorality. (1 Thessalonians 4:3)

The body is not meant for sexual immorality but for the Lord, and the Lord for the body.... Do you not know that your bodies are members of Christ himself? Shall I then take the members of Christ and unite them with a prostitute? Never! Do you not know that he who unites himself with a prostitute is one with her in body? For it is said, "The two will become one flesh." But he who unites himself with the Lord is one with him in spirit.

Flee from sexual immorality. All other sins a man commits are outside his body, but he who sins sexually sins against his own body. Do you not know that your body is a temple of the Holy Spirit, who is in you, whom you have received from God? You are not your own; you were bought at a price. Therefore honor God with your body. (1 Corinthians 6:13–20)

Put to death, therefore, whatever belongs to your earthly nature:

sexual immorality, impurity, lust, evil desires and greed, which is idolatry. Because of these, the wrath of God is coming. You used to walk in these ways, in the life you once lived. But now you must rid yourselves of all such things. (Colossians 3:5–8)

But among you there must not be even a hint of sexual immorality, or of any kind of impurity, or of greed, because these are improper for God's holy people. Nor should there be obscenity, foolish talk or coarse joking, which are out of place, but rather thanksgiving. For of this you can be sure: No immoral, impure or greedy person—such a man is an idolater—has any inheritance in the kingdom of Christ and of God. (Ephesians 5:3–5)

Do not be yoked together with unbelievers. For what do righteousness and wickedness have in common? Or what fellowship can light have with darkness? (2 Corinthians 6:14)

"You have heard that it was said, 'Do not commit adultery,' But I tell you that anyone who looks at a woman lustfully has already committed adultery with her in his heart." (Matthew 5:27–28)

We demolish arguments and every pretension that sets itself up against the knowledge of God, and we take captive every thought to make it obedient to Christ. (2 Corinthians 10:5)

Steps TO TAKE

1. Sit in stillness and let God speak to you.
2. Pray: Lord, I ask You forgiveness for _____.
Give me Your power to change _____.
Give me Your plan to prevent sinning like this again. With Your strength I intend to live in chastity. God, I give my future plans to You. Lord, fill my thoughts with You. I receive Your power to reject the unclean thoughts the devil keeps throwing at me.
3. Meditate on the greatness of God, who gives His commands for your good and can keep you from falling.

Respect for Authority

The Lord knows how to rescue godly men from trials and to hold the unrighteous for the day of judgment, while continuing their punishment. This is especially true of those who follow the corrupt desire of the sinful nature and *despise authority*. (2 Peter 2:9–10, italics mine)

If a man curses his father or mother, his lamp will be snuffed out in pitch darkness. (Proverbs 20:20)

Honor your father and your mother, so that you may live long in the land the Lord your God is giving you. (Exodus 20:12)

Listen to your father, who gave you life, and do not despise your mother when she is old. Buy the truth and do not sell it; get wisdom, discipline and understanding. The father of a righteous man has great joy; he who has a wise son delights in him. May your father and mother be glad; may she who gave you birth rejoice! (Proverbs 23:22–25)

Obey your leaders and submit to their authority. They keep watch over you as men who must give an account. Obey them so that their work will be a joy, not a burden, for that would be of no advantage to you. (Hebrews 13:17)

Everyone must submit himself to the governing authorities, for there is no authority except that which God has established. The authorities that exist have been established by God. Consequently, he who rebels against the authority is rebelling against what God has instituted, and those who do so will bring judgment on themselves. For rulers hold no terror for those who do right, but for those who do wrong. Do you want to be free from fear of the one in authority? Then do what is right and he will commend you. For he is God's servant to do you good. But if you do wrong, be afraid, for he does not bear the sword for nothing. He is God's servant, an agent of wrath to bring punishment on the wrongdoer. Therefore, it is necessary to submit to the authorities, not only because of possible punishment but also because of conscience. This is also why you pay taxes, for the authorities are God's servants, who give their full time to governing. Give everyone what you owe him: If you owe taxes, pay taxes; if revenue, then revenue; if respect, then respect, if honor, then honor. (Romans 13:1–7)

The king's heart is in the hand of the Lord; he directs it like a watercourse wherever he pleases. (Proverbs 21:1)

Commit your way to the Lord; trust in him and he will do this: He will make your righteousness shine like the dawn, and justice of your cause like the noonday sun. (Psalm 37:5–6)

Do not take revenge, my friends, but leave room for God's wrath, for it is written: "It is mine to avenge; I will repay," says the Lord. (Romans 12:19)

Steps TO TAKE

1. Silently permit God to speak to you.
2. Pray: Lord, I never realized that respect for authority was such a big deal with You. I confess _____ and _____ as sin and ask for Your forgiveness. Please yank out that deep-down rebellion by the roots. I know it will hurt, but I've got to get rid of it. I receive Your grace to respect authority—not only outwardly but inwardly. _____ and _____ are things I must change. When authority is unfair, I rely on Your power and justice to bail me out.
3. Focus your thinking on God, who is so awesome that He has used Pharaoh, Cyrus (the Persian king who allowed the Jews to return to their land after their captivity in Babylon), and even Pilate, to work out His purposes. Unless you receive an order that directly contradicts God's Word, obey authority and let God stick up for your rights.

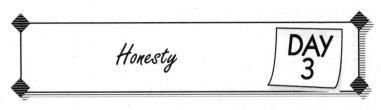

Lord, who may dwell in your sanctuary? Who may live on your holy hill? He whose walk is blameless and who does what is righteous, who speaks the truth from his heart and has no slander on his tongue, who does his neighbor no wrong and casts no slur on his fellow man...who keeps his oath even when it hurts. (Psalm 15:1–4)

Surely you desire truth in the inner parts. (Psalm 51:6)

To do what is right and just is more acceptable to the Lord than sacrifice. (Proverbs 21:3)

The integrity of the upright guides them, but the unfaithful are destroyed by their duplicity. (Proverbs 11:3)

He whose walk is upright fears the Lord, but he whose ways are devious despises him. (Proverbs 14:2)

All a man's ways seem innocent to him, but motives are weighed by the Lord. (Proverbs 16:2)

Be careful to do what is right in the eyes of everybody. (Romans 12:17)

[The apostle Paul speaking] We want to avoid any criticism of the way we administer this liberal gift. For we are taking pains to do what is right, not only in the eyes of the Lord but also in the eyes of men. (2 Corinthians 8:20–21)

You must have accurate and honest weights and measures, so that you may live long in the land the Lord your God is giving you. For the Lord your God detests . . . anyone who deals dishonestly . . . (Deuteronomy 25:15–16)

A false witness will not go unpunished, and he who pours out lies will perish. (Proverbs 19:9)

Do not lie to each other, since you have taken off your old self with its practices. (Colossians 3:9)

Therefore each of you must put off falsehood and speak truthfully to his neighbor.... He who has been stealing must steal no longer, but must work, doing something with his own hands, that he may have something to share with those in need. (Ephesians 4:25, 28)

Serve wholeheartedly, as if you were serving the Lord, not men, because you know that the Lord will reward everyone for whatever good he does, whether he is slave or free. (Ephesians 6:7–8)

Make it your ambition to lead a quiet life, to mind your own business and to work with your hands, just as we told you, so that your daily life may win the respect of outsiders. (1 Thessalonians 4:11–12)

Steps TO TAKE

1. As you read and reread these passages, sit in silence as you wait for God to speak to you.

2. Pray: Lord, show me Yourself, and give me a deep appreciation of Your awesome holiness. I know that as Your child I am to be holy just like You. I realize that _____ and _____ are wrong, and I determine to change. I want to be transparently honest so that my testimony won't be tarnished. I will continually ask You to evaluate my motives. Spend time worshiping the Lord "in the splendor of his holiness" (Psalm 29:2).

Processing Pride — DAY 4

Young men [and women], in the same way be submissive to those who are older. All of you, clothe yourselves with humility toward one another, because, "God opposes the proud but gives grace to the humble." Humble yourselves, therefore, under God's mighty hand, that he may lift you up in due time. (1 Peter 5:5–6)

The Lord detests the proud of heart. Be sure of this: They will not go unpunished. (Proverbs 16:5)

Pride goes before destruction, a haughty spirit before a fall. (Proverbs 16:18)

Before a downfall a man's heart is proud, but humility comes before honor. (Proverbs 18:12)

When pride comes, then comes disgrace, but with humility comes wisdom. (Proverbs 11:2)

A man's pride brings him low, but a man of lowly spirit gains honor. (Proverbs 29:23)

Pride only breeds quarrels, but wisdom is found in those who take advice. (Proverbs 13:10)

Do not be proud, but be willing to associate with people of low position. Do not be conceited. (Romans 12:16)

...as the king was walking on the roof of the royal palace of Babylon, he said, "Is not this the great Babylon I have built as the royal residence, by my mighty power and for the glory of my majesty?" The words were still on his lips when a voice came from heaven, "This is what is decreed for you, King Nebuchadnezzar: Your royal authority has been taken from you. You will be driven away from people and will live with the wild animals." (Daniel 4:29–32)

Then Hezekiah repented of the pride of his heart, as did the people of Jerusalem; therefore the Lord's wrath did not come upon them during the days of Hezekiah. (2 Chronicles 32:26)

Humble yourselves before the Lord, and he will lift you up. (James 4:10)

"For whoever exalts himself will be humbled, and whoever humbles himself will be exalted." (Matthew 23:12)

For this is what the high and lofty One says—he who lives forever, whose name is holy: "I live in a high and holy place, but also with him who is contrite and lowly in spirit, to revive the spirit of the lowly and to revive the heart of the contrite." (Isaiah 57:15)

He has showed you, O man [woman], what is good. And what does the Lord require of you? To act justly and to love mercy and to walk humbly with your God. (Micah 6:8)

Steps TO TAKE

1. In stillness let God speak to your heart.
2. Pray: Dear God, I often forget that *You* know it all and I act as

if I do! Please forgive me for being so arrogant. I need to learn to listen to others and to You. A Nebuchadnezzar-like humbling experience is something I'd rather live without, so I want to take steps to avoid it. I want to humble myself before You. Help me to always heed the warnings You give me about pride.

3. Consider the wisdom and power of God. Compare that with your mistakes and your weaknesses. Then humble yourself before Him.

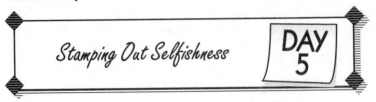

Stamping Out Selfishness **DAY 5**

For we know that our old self was crucified with him so that the body of sin might be done away with, that we should no longer be slaves to sin. (Romans 6:6)

We died to sin; how can we live in it any longer? (Romans 6:2)

In the same way, count yourselves dead to sin but alive to God in Christ Jesus. (Romans 6:11)

I have been crucified with Christ and I no longer live, but Christ lives in me. The life I live in the body, I live by faith of the Son of God, who loved me and gave himself for me. (Galatians 2:20)

He himself bore our sins in his body on the tree, so that we might die to sins and live for righteousness. (1 Peter 2:24)

Do nothing out of selfish ambition or vain conceit, but in humility consider others better than yourselves. Each of you should look not only to your own interests, but also to the interests of others. (Philippians 2:3–4)

Be devoted to one another in brotherly love. Honor one another above yourselves. (Romans 12:10)

"If anyone would come after me, he must deny himself and take up his cross daily and follow me. For whoever wants to save his life will lose it, but whoever loses his life for me will save it." (Luke 9:23–24)

"So in everything, do to others what you would have them do to you, for this sums up the Law and the Prophets." (Matthew 7:12)

"But I tell you, Do not resist an evil person. If someone strikes you on the right cheek, turn to him the other also. And if someone wants to sue you and take your tunic, let him have your cloak as well. If someone forces you to go one mile, go with him two miles. Give to the one who asks you, and do not turn away from the one who wants to borrow from you." (Matthew 5:39–42)

1. As you sit silently before Him meditating on these verses, let God speak to you.

2. Pray: Lord, I know I'm rather spoiled and enjoy getting my own way. Thank You, Jesus, that through Your death on the cross You won the victory over sin. That means because You live in me and I am in You, my selfishness is a conquered enemy—if only I depend on Your power and treat it as such. Of course I can let it out of its cage if I choose, but in Your strength I can put others above myself. Lord, receiving Your resources, I determine to remain unselfish even when

_____

and _____.

I will renounce my selfishness to live wholeheartedly for You and for others.

3. Reflect on the selfless life Jesus lived. Decide how you can follow His example.

Chapter Five
The Troubled Teen Survival Kit

Elizabeth struggled to make it through another lackluster day. It was the same unrelenting routine: classes, making French fries at McDonald's, math homework, washing a load of clothes so she'd have something to wear the next day, watching her favorite TV show—and trying to figure out how she could get some nice guy to like her. Surveying the mess that "Hurricane Elizabeth" had perpetrated on her room, she wondered when she'd ever be able to clean it up and mentally rehearsed what she'd answer when her mother got on her case. On Saturday, it would be no better: she worked in the morning, had play practice in the afternoon, and had to find time to come up with a way to organize her committee to decorate for the youth group party in the evening. Her mom had decreed that attendance was required at Sunday's family reunion, and Monday the outline for her term paper was due. She felt doomed to finish the week exhausted, and start the next one the same way.

It was much too late when she finally turned off the light and crawled into bed. Instead of falling asleep immediately, she spent some time worrying about how she would get everything done. When her alarm rang, she just didn't feel ready to face another day—but then it seemed as if everyone else ran the rat race just like she did.

Her mom held down a full-time job, kept an immaculate house, and

had overcommitted herself at church. The price seemed to be constant fatigue, tension headaches, and insomnia. Her father put in long hours at the office. He was the boss and everything in the growing business depended on him. When he got home he preferred the newspaper and the television to his family. He was just too tired to talk to anybody, much less take an interest in Elizabeth's activities. Her sister was a straight-*A* student, but had to drop out of college for a semester because she couldn't take the pressure. But, Elizabeth reasoned, it was better to be a *yuppie* than a bum.

Elizabeth, like so many people, blamed the fast pace of modern life for the hectic weirdness of her existence. Sometimes she felt that, as a Christian, she should be able to experience more peace. Yet she had no evidence that the lives of the other families at church were any different.

Elizabeth attended a Christian school and her English teacher required that they make several book reports on biographies of great Christians. She found the reading fascinating. She also began to question her theory that it was the modern world that made life so stressful. Hudson Taylor had traveled to China on a ship that was nearly dashed to pieces by a terrible storm, and he arrived—in the middle of a war—only to find that there was no one to meet him and that the money promised for his support had not arrived. This sounded a lot more hairy than school assignments and working at McDonald's.

Maria Taylor, Hudson's wife, had to cope with threats of exotic diseases and attacks from fanatical mobs, which forced her to send her children to England for a time. Besides being a wife and mother who moved frequently, she helped watch over some of the women missionaries, evangelized, and taught Bible classes. The lives of her mother and sister were soft by comparison.

Elizabeth also read of David Livingstone, who literally walked across most of Africa, not knowing if a lion, a hyena, or a cannibal might choose him for supper. Usually, he had no one to talk to, no chance for recreation, and no word from his family. No medical care would be available if he got sick, and he had no place to call home. Somehow driving in rush-hour traffic, facing dateless Saturday nights, or having to microwave leftovers and eat alone hardly belonged in the same category.

Mary Slessor was another person who intrigued Elizabeth. She had left Scotland as a single missionary to one of the darkest parts of

Africa. The heathenism, disease, and danger were too much for some, who broke under the strain—but not for Mary. Elizabeth wondered if she could have lasted two weeks in a similar situation.

She wouldn't have traded places with Martin Luther either. While some threatened his life, his loyal followers forced on him a role of leadership and church organization that was incredibly demanding. In forming a new church, he did everything from writing new songs, to improving the translation of the Bible, to trying to bring quarreling factions of society together.

As Elizabeth read about more "spiritual giants," she began to realize that each one lived life with an inner tranquility that integrated their daily activities. None of them rushed frantically from one thing to another, operating in constant frustration or zooming into frequent despair. And it wasn't because they enjoyed smooth sailing, encountered favorable circumstances, or were unusually rich and talented. They all started out as very ordinary people: George Muller, who prayed in all the money needed to support thousands of orphans, began as a college partier and playboy. David Brainerd, the great missionary to the North American Indians, was an orphan. Corrie ten Boom, who worked to save Jews during World War II, was a single lady who worked in her father's watch shop and taught a little Sunday school class for retarded children. Most of them lived through hardships Elizabeth couldn't even identify with.

It slowly dawned on her that each of them possessed the same secret: *They knew how to enjoy the Lord's presence, and they spent peaceful time with God each day.*

Elizabeth had always thought of prayer only as "something every Christian should be engaged in so the world can be changed," "storming the gates of heaven in order to receive things from God," and "spiritual warfare against the hosts of darkness." Now Elizabeth began to see that there were two distinct aspects to prayer: (1) the restful part of it, thanking and praising God and enjoying His presence, (2) the work side of prayer, or intercession, which included asking God for the things we need and praying for individuals, families, churches, governments, and nations. Although Elizabeth's newfound heroes were also good at intercession, she wanted to learn more about their sweet intimacy with God.

About Hudson Taylor she read: "In England he had learned the value of spending the first hour of the day in prayer and communication with God. This became the resolute pattern of his life in China."[1] If he was staying in a Chinese inn and sharing a room with many people, he'd wake up in the middle of the night, light a candle to read a portion of Scripture, spend time in prayer, and then fall back asleep. David Livingstone died on his knees in prayer. Mary Slessor had learned to let the peace of God invade her heart in every situation. She wrote: "I am not very particular about my bed these days, but as I lay on a few dirty sticks laid across and covered with a litter of dirty corn shells, with plenty of rats and insects, three women and an infant three days old alongside, and over a dozen sheep and goats and cows outside, you don't wonder that I slept little. But I had such a comfortable quiet night in my own heart."[2] Martin Luther was a man who knew how to converse with God. Beginning each day with three hours of private prayer, Martin Luther was an expert at communicating with God.[3] When Corrie ten Boom came to the Lord, it was evident that she had something special going with Him. Each morning, George Muller walked for an hour or two as he prayed.

☑ A Secret for Stressed-Out Students

Even people with no Christian roots realize that we need solitude, time to fix our minds on something different than our daily routine, and rest with a spiritual emphasis. That necessity can only be truly filled by contact with God himself. The counterfeits are, at best, superficial and some can be downright dangerous. Activities range from spending time in nature, or participating in various cultural experiences, to Eastern meditation, and taking drugs to "expand the mind."

A friend of mine, Jewell Erickson, did a lot of research on stress control and she arrived at the following conclusion:

> Stress has been defined as the "wear and tear of life." It comes both from outside and inside ourselves—"conflicts without and fears within" (2 Corinthians 7:5). Discussing things with another person is a time-honored therapy. Talking to God is like talking to your best friend, but because He is not a mere mortal He will never misunderstand you. He is always available, and He is able to move heaven and earth to help you. Pouring our joys and sorrows out to Him can bring great release of mind and spirit."

---

[1]Colin Whittaker, *Seven Guides to Effective Prayer* (Minneapolis: Bethany House Publishers, 1987), p. 68.
[2]Gordon MacDonald, *Ordering Your Private World* (Nashville: Oliver Nelson, 1985), p. 24.
[3]Mike Fearon, *Martin Luther* (Minneapolis: Bethany House Publishers, 1986), p. 156.

Drawing near to God in wordless prayer and then listening for His perspective will bring the peace we need to calm the troubled waters of our lives.

The neat thing about following the Lord's design of giving Him our time is that the only gift we can present to God is also the component that brings purpose, peace, and emotional stability. Inward calm enables us to spend our lives for other people without burning out. We need quiet time each day when we can meet with God to praise and worship and receive from Him. Used only as an escape, it can degenerate into a mysticism that can become rather weird. Correctly applied, it makes God's children capable of living in a crazy world with the goal of helping mixed-up people. Ignoring our inner life with God produces apathetic comfort-zone addicts or frazzled fretting do-gooders.

The *Westminster Shorter Catechism* declares: "The chief end of man is to love God and to enjoy Him forever." John 17:3 records the words of Jesus as He talked with His Father: "Now this is eternal life; that they may know you, the only true God, and Jesus Christ, whom you have sent." Knowing God begins with salvation—but all of us, like Abraham, are called to become friends of God. Expressing our love to God, basking in His presence, praising and thanking Him—and just *enjoying* time with Him! These things should be as natural to a Christian as breathing. As we spend this intimate time with God, we sense joy, fulfillment, and relaxation because we were created especially for this. Recreation has its place in a healthy lifestyle, but attending a football game, going to the beach, or playing a video game won't accomplish the same thing in your life as quality time with God when your spirit really touches His. You can come home from vacation all worn out, but you'll emerge from God's presence refreshed and renewed.

How does a person learn to meet God in a real way? It's not easy. Like building any solid relationship, it will take time and effort. People conditioned by our activity-centered society will think it strange that you "give up" a TV show, pizza with your friends, or sleeping-in so you can spend time with God. But you'll never be able to love God by obeying Him if you don't sit still and listen to His voice. You'll not be able to deal effectively with chaos and tension without permitting God to restructure your daily priorities.

Learning to meet God each day will be one of the biggest challenges of your life and it will be the most worthwhile!

YOU HAVE AN APPOINTMENT WITH THE CREATOR OF THE UNIVERSE...

...to learn how some of His characteristics can rub off on you!

If You Need it, God's Got It

No *technique* will ever form a relationship, but some of these strategies can help you to learn how to spend time with God.

Love That Lasts Forever   DAY 1

But God demonstrates his own love for us in this: While we were still sinners, Christ died for us. (Romans 5:8)

As a father has compassion on his children, so the Lord has compassion on those who fear him; for he knows how we are formed, he remembers that we are dust. (Psalm 103:13–14)

The Lord appeared to us in the past, saying: "I have loved you with an everlasting love; I have drawn you with loving-kindness." (Jeremiah 31:3)

No, in all these things we are more than conquerors through him who loved us. For I am convinced that neither death nor life, neither angels nor demons, neither the present nor the future, nor any power, neither height nor depth, nor anything else in all creation, will be able to separate us from the love of God that is in Christ Jesus our Lord. (Romans 8:37–39)

God is love. Whoever lives in love lives in God, and God in him.... There is no fear in love. But perfect love drives out fear. (1 John 4:16, 18)

1. Tell God out loud how much you love Him, explaining in detail why He means so much to you. Receive the love of One who died for you and keeps on loving you whether or not you deserve it. Enjoy the compassion and understanding that's part of a true Father's love. Realize that God's love is forever—no matter what you've said or done or plan for the future. Grasp the fact that nothing—your being rejected by other people, a terrible home life, a friend who proved to be a traitor, or the results of your sin or that of others—absolutely nothing can separate you from God's love. Give your fears to God and let Him replace them with His love.

2. Reread the verses and jot down the thoughts God gives you.

_____

_____

_____

_____

_____

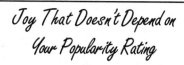 

*Joy That Doesn't Depend on
Your Popularity Rating*

DAY 2

You have made known to me the path of life; you will fill me with joy in your presence, with eternal pleasures at your right hand. (Psalm 16:11)

"If you obey my commands, you will remain in my love, just as I have obeyed my Father's commands and remain in his love. I have told you this so that my joy may be in you and that your joy might be complete." (John 15:10–11)

[Jesus, praying to His Father]: "I am coming to you now, but I say these things while I am still in the world, so that they may have the full measure of my joy within them." (John 17:13)

...the joy of the Lord is your strength. (Nehemiah 8:10)

Rejoice in the Lord always. I will say it again: Rejoice! (Philippians 4:4)

How priceless is your unfailing love! Both high and low among men find refuge in the shadow of your wings. They feast on the abundance of your house; you give them drink from your river of delights. For with you is the fountain of life; in your light we see light. (Psalm 36:7–9)

Steps TO TAKE

1. Ask God to wrap you up in His presence. Experience the closeness of Jesus that can melt away the tears, the anxiety, the frustration, and the boredom that robs you of contentment. If you remain before God in expectation long enough, the eye of calm will appear even within life's most horrible hurricane. Realize that flowing with the com-

mandments of Jesus—obeying them and not resisting them—is the secret to joy. If some disobedience is robbing you of peace with God, now is the time to make things right.

2. Receive the full measure of the joy of Christ. Joy comes from Him, and has nothing to do with some frantic search for happiness. Just look to Jesus. When your eyes are completely fixed on Him, joy will spring up from within. Permit God-given, deep-down contentment to provide you with stamina and enthusiasm even when the going gets tough.

3. Find security in that secret place with God, where there are unending spiritual delights. Revel in the quiet ecstasy of knowing you are loved and cared for by the Maker of the universe. He is your never-ending source of joy.

4. Read the verses again noting the thoughts God brings to your mind. _____

_____

_____

_____

_____

5. Take the time to feast on His abundance and drink from His river of delights. Let Jesus be your joy. If you do, a bad grade, a spat with a friend, or a fender-bender accident can't ruin your day. You can just go back to Jesus for a new supply of joy.

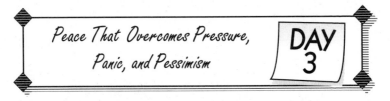

Peace That Overcomes Pressure, Panic, and Pessimism

DAY 3

Therefore, since we have been justified through faith, we have peace with God through our Lord Jesus Christ. (Romans 5:1)

The mind of sinful man is death, but the mind controlled by the Spirit is life and peace. (Romans 8:6)

[Jesus' words] "Peace I leave with you; my peace I give you. I do not give to you as the world gives. Do not let your hearts be troubled, and do not be afraid." (John 14:27)

You will keep in perfect peace him who is steadfast, because he trusts in you. (Isaiah 26:3)

Great peace have they who love your law, and nothing can make them stumble. (Psalm 119:165)

May the God of hope fill you with all joy and peace as you trust in him, so that you may overflow with hope by the power of the Holy Spirit. (Romans 15:13)

Do not be anxious about anything, but in everything, by prayer and petition, with thanksgiving, present your requests to God. And the peace of God, which transcends all understanding, will guard your hearts and your minds in Christ Jesus. (Philippians 4:6-7)

Let the peace of Christ rule in your hearts, since as members of one body you were called to peace. And be thankful. (Colossians 3:15)

Now may the Lord of peace himself give you peace at all times and in every way. (2 Thessalonians 3:16)

Steps TO TAKE

1. Thank God for His wonderful salvation, and for the indwelling Holy Spirit who can guide your thoughts and actions in accordance with His will—which always results in peace with Him. Ask God for the gift of His peace in the troubled areas of your life. Fix your gaze on God and the way He views your problems from His *all-powerful, all-knowing,* and *everywhere-present* perspective.

2. Pray about the difficult situations in your life with authority and thanksgiving, receiving the coolness and the beauty of God's peace. Make it a point to reject all the disturbing thoughts the devil throws at you in order to let the peace of Christ rule in your heart.

3. Reread the verses, writing down the thoughts God gives you.

80

Patience, Perseverance, Endurance— Whatever You Call It — DAY 4

Consider it pure joy, my brothers, whenever you face trials of many kinds, because you know that the testing of your faith develops perseverance. Perseverance must finish its work so that you may be mature and complete, not lacking anything. (James 1:2–4)

Not only so, but we also rejoice in our sufferings, because we know that suffering produces perseverance; perseverance, character; and character, hope. And hope does not disappoint us, because God has poured out his love into our hearts by the Holy Spirit, whom he has given us. (Romans 5:3–5)

For this very reason, make every effort to add to your faith goodness; and to goodness, knowledge; and to knowledge, self-control; and to self-control, perseverance; and to perseverance, godliness; and to godliness, brotherly kindness; and to brotherly kindness, love. For if you possess these qualities in increasing measure, they will keep you from being ineffective and unproductive in your knowledge of our Lord Jesus Christ. (2 Peter 1:5–8)

We want each of you to show this same diligence to the very end, in order to make your hope sure. We do not want you to become lazy, but to imitate those who through faith and patience inherit what has been promised. (Hebrews 6:11–12)

So do not throw away your confidence; it will be richly rewarded. You need to persevere so that when you have done the will of God, you will receive what he has promised. (Hebrews 10:35–36)

Therefore, since we are surrounded by such a great cloud of witnesses, let us throw off everything that hinders and the sin that so easily entangles, and let us run with perseverance the race marked out for us. Let us fix our eyes on Jesus, the author and perfecter of our faith. (Hebrews 12:1–2)

But you, man of God, flee from all this, and pursue righteousness, godliness, faith, love, endurance and gentleness. (1 Timothy 6:11)

Steps TO TAKE

1. Thank God for His purpose in suffering. Check in with God and revise the attitudes you have toward the trials you're presently facing.

2. Ask God to show you your part in making the patience-producing process more effective in your life. Submit your I-feel-like-quitting feelings to God, allowing Him to replace them with His patience and perseverance.

3. As you prayerfully read through the passages again write down the things God impresses on your heart.

_____

_____

_____

_____

_____

_____

Contagious Kindness— Spreading the Epidemic

DAY 5

The Lord is gracious and compassionate, slow to anger and rich in love. The Lord is good to all; he has compassion on all he has made. (Psalm 145:8–9)

When [Jesus] saw the crowds, he had compassion on them... because they were... like sheep without a shepherd. (Matthew 9:36)

[Jesus speaking] "I have compassion for these people; they have already been with me three days and have nothing to eat." (Mark 8:2)

Add to your faith, goodness; and to goodness, knowledge; and to knowledge, self-control; and to self-control, perseverance; and to perseverance, godliness; and to godliness, brotherly kindness, and to brotherly kindness, love. (2 Peter 1:5–7)

Be kind and compassionate to one another, forgiving each other, just as in Christ God forgave you. (Ephesians 4:32)

Love is patient, love is kind. It does not envy, it does not boast, it is not proud. (1 Corinthians 13:4)

Therefore, as God's chosen people, holy and dearly loved, clothe yourselves with compassion, kindness, humility, gentleness and patience. Bear with each other and forgive whatever grievances you may have against one another. (Colossians 3:12–13)

Finally, all of you, live in harmony with one another; be sympathetic, love as brothers, be compassionate and humble. Do not repay evil with evil or insult with insult, but with blessing. (1 Peter 3:8–9)

Therefore, as we have opportunity, let us do good to all people, especially to those who belong to the family of believers. (Galatians 6:10)

I want to stress these things, so that those who have trusted in God may be careful to devote themselves to doing what is good. These things are excellent and profitable for everyone. (Titus 3:8)

If anyone has material possessions and sees his brother in need but has no pity on him, how can the love of God be in him. (1 John 3:17)

Do nothing out of selfish ambition or vain conceit, but in humility consider others better than yourselves. (Philippians 2:3)

Be devoted to one another in brotherly love. Honor one another above yourselves... Share with God's people who are in need. Practice hospitality. (Romans 12:10, 13)

Steps TO TAKE

1. Get a new look at the God of all compassion and just take in His kindness and His mercy. Meditate on the fact that true Christian kindness comes from the heart of God and is not something you drum up because it's expected of you. Ask God to show you how true kindness is connected to faith, knowledge, perseverance, and godliness. Receive

from God the kindness He wishes to show to others through you.

2. Permit Him to remove any *getting-rid-of-a-guilty-conscience-do-goodism* that may reside in you. Receive His forgiveness for all sin and His motives for all your actions. Let God give you *His* blueprint for showing specific kindnesses to others this week.

3. Reread the verses, jotting down the thoughts God gives you.

_____

_____

_____

_____

_____

4. Using a concordance, find the word *goodness*. Then look up each verse listed and, following the pattern used for the first five fruits of the Spirit, meditate upon it and receive what God has for you. Do the same for the other fruits of the Spirit—faithfulness, gentleness, and self-control.

Chapter Six
Pray With Your Life

Amy got off the school bus and walked up the short driveway to their farmhouse. Defeated and discouraged, she failed to appreciate the crisp, clear fall air, the oak leaves set aglow by the sunshine, or the golden yellow of the chrysanthemums her mother had planted inside a big tractor tire. Their collie, Rusty, barked his welcome, and Amy laid down her books to pet him a little. But she was still condemning herself for what she'd done that day.

Once inside, she plopped into the big chair and sat there motionless. She was glad her mom wasn't home to ask her what was wrong. She probably would have answered—*everything*. Reliving her day, Amy put a *D-* on her Christian report card: When breakfast wasn't ready on time, she'd snapped at her mother. While she waited, she bawled out her little brother for borrowing her volleyball. During first hour, she'd joined in with everyone making fun of Mrs. Sikorski behind her back. At the lunch table, Ellen had confided, "I'd commit suicide, but I'm afraid to die." Amy's palms became sweaty and her voice faltered as she sputtered, "You don't have to be. Jesus can..." Just then Julie joined them, and Amy chickened out of witnessing for Christ. Then, on the bus, Joe announced that he had a dirty joke to tell if no one objected. Amy hadn't had the courage to say anything and she felt guilty.

Amy usually had her daily devotions when she came home from school each day. Because her mother worked and her brother always went to Grandma's house it was a good time to be alone. She began by telling God how sorry she was for letting Him down. Then she absent-mindedly flipped her Bible open to Matthew 10. "Anyone who loves his father or mother more than me is not worthy of me; anyone who loves son or daughter more than me is not worthy of me; and anyone who does not take his cross and follow me is not worthy of me." The words hit her with unusual force. She knew that in the "Amy Anderson Revised Standard Version" it would read: "Anyone who loves popularity more than me is not worthy of me." She realized that just telling God she felt bad about her sins wasn't enough: She had to surrender her desire to be admired by others to God and be willing to suffer persecution, or shame, or teasing for the name of Jesus. She simply prayed, "Okay Lord, I give in. I'm willing to be considered weird for You. Amen."

Because she had only a half-hour's worth of homework and all evening to do it, she picked up the biography of Hudson Taylor her mother was reading. Scanning the chapter titles she saw, "Days of Darkness." It fit her mood, and she began reading. To her surprise, she discovered that this great missionary to China had also felt the same feeling of failure that plagued her now.

The next chapter, entitled "The Exchanged Life," made her curious. There she found an amazing passage: "The Lord Jesus received is holiness begun; the Lord Jesus cherished is holiness advancing, the Lord Jesus counted on as never absent would be holiness complete."[1] The chapter went on to explain how Hudson Taylor's spiritual eyes were opened and how his constant striving was replaced by total rest in Jesus at all times. His life changed so drastically that everyone noticed.

Amy really wanted that kind of life—but it seemed too simple. What about all the "growing in grace" she'd always heard about? She turned to the verse she'd memorized: "But grow in the grace and the knowledge of our Lord and Savior Jesus Christ" (2 Peter 3:18). She had always assumed that growing in grace was *her* responsibility. Slowly it dawned on her: If you plant something in the right soil, it grows automatically. Like any farm girl, Amy could appreciate the miracle of growth.

The grace and knowledge of Jesus is the *soil* in which we can grow as Christians, and it is super soil. Her pastor's definition of grace was "favor, kindness, friendship, and God's forgiving mercy." By spending time in the Word and in prayer she could improve the soil, but God would take care of the growth.

Just as the roots of a plant receive nutrients from the soil, we are to *receive* all the good things God has to offer us. As a plant is totally dependent on the ground for growth, so we can only rest in Jesus and trust Him to produce in us the qualities of a true Christian. Jesus described it as a branch abiding in a vine.

Wow, thought Amy, *it's all Jesus from beginning to end—not my endless introspection, worry, and striving.* The words of a recent sermon came back to her, "Knowing Jesus comes from spending time meditating on His words and sensing His presence. The closer you grow to another person, the more you learn about him or her. Really get to know the one who died for you. Jesus is all you need." These words now had real meaning. She was beginning to understand that an

---

[1]Dr. and Mrs. Howard Taylor, *Hudson Taylor's Spiritual Secret*, p. 155.

all-powerful Jesus had tons of love, joy, peace, meekness, courage, kindness, and ability to sympathize with Mrs. Sikorski—if Amy was open to receive and had no unsurrendered desires to clog the channel.

Amy just whispered, "Lord, give me the miracle of Jesus, living the Christian life through me."

When we really count on the resurrected all-powerful Jesus as never absent and always ready to help us, our lives change. No longer are there some compartments for God and others for self, because God permeates our entire being. There's a new freedom in doing what God asks of us. Your life turns into one constant conversation with God. Giving to Him and receiving from Him becomes as natural as breathing.

I really think that the command of 1 Thessalonians 5:17—"pray continually"—means that you pray with your *life*. You can constantly submit to God by saying, "Your will be done," even when you don't particularly feel like obeying your parents or going to church on Sunday night. Moment by moment you acknowledge His powerful presence to overcome the temptation, to still the storm that keeps your emotions in turmoil, or to give you power to obey God even when the cost is very great.

O. Hallesby once said, "True praying is to ask the risen Christ to come in."[2] When you really believe that Jesus is right there with you to handle the situation, things change. Faith that God will supernaturally supply, even when things look hopeless, means you never "need" anything sinful.

Four times the Bible explains, "The righteous will live by faith" (Romans 1:17; Habakkuk 2:4; Galatians 3:11; Hebrews 10:38). It's important to realize that either you go it on your own, or in faith you reach out for God's power to overcome. There is a beautiful joy in discovering that a life of victory over sin *is* possible—that sin isn't a necessity with which you must coexist. But righteousness is only *received*—first of all by having a saving faith, and then by the daily faith that invites Jesus into every detail of life.

This quality of spiritual life is described in different ways and given different names—full surrender, victorious Christian living, spiritual breathing, sanctification, and realizing your death and resurrection with Jesus. These are just some of the expressions used. Each of them includes these three elements:

1. Accept the biblical definition of God and the scriptural standard of right and wrong instead of personal feelings and rationalization.

2. Constantly affirm either in a verbalized form or with an unspoken attitude, the prayer: "Your will be done." The Bible commands: "...count yourselves dead to sin but alive to God in Christ Jesus" (Romans 6:11).

3. Realize that in your own strength you can't obey God, but that by faith you can receive His power to do the right thing. If you've surrendered every desire to Him and count on the power and wisdom of the risen Christ in each situation, there is no reason to lie to save face or to compromise your testimony to make a good impression.

Living in the victory of continual prayer by an attitude of faith—knowing that Jesus will always come through—is to experience Romans 8:2: "Because through Christ Jesus the law of the Spirit of life set me free from the law of sin and death."

Sure it's "natural" to sin—but the Christian has the option of rising into the supernatural where, by faith, we rely on the power of Christ.

---

[2]Douglas F. Kelly, Ph.D., *Why Pray?* (Brentwood, Tennessee: Wolgemuth & Hyatt Publishers, Inc., 1989), p. 40.

Living this abundant life makes us sort of like airplanes, which overcome the law of gravity by the higher law of aerodynamics. But just because we learn to fly doesn't mean we'll never encounter another problem.

There are several things that could ground any pilot. A sudden panic attack could make him decide that flying was impossible. Attempting to fly a plane with a defective design would prove futile. Turning off the automatic controls and warning systems to use his "superior instincts" to maneuver through the fog, any pilot, no matter how experienced, could manage to crash. Without an adequate fuel supply, a forced landing will be necessary.

The supernatural power system to overcome temptation is available to every Christian. However, many never use it! Some don't even realize it's there. Some lose it completely because of a sin they refuse to give up. Others, although they do revert back to trusting themselves at times, basically put *the-just-shall-live-by-faith* principle into practice. No one has *perfect* faith so that they *never* falter and stumble into sinful behavior. But the Christian who has learned to trust God for supernatural power, and who immediately confesses any sin so he or she can fly again, has discovered the abundant life that Jesus offers.

Decide by faith to plug into the Jesus power system, to receive all the gifts of the Spirit that God has for you and, once and for all, to give the control of your life over to God. Learn how to overcome the obstacles Satan will put in your way. If you do fall, confess and forsake your sin, learn from your mistake, and again come to Jesus to receive His power.

The devil will try to tell you that victory over some particular sin is impossible. Once you listen to his twenty-six reasons why you must accept defeat and believe them, you're finished. Another favorite trick of his is getting you to ignore or rationalize Scriptures. For example, if you always read comforting Bible passages and never even look at the Ten Commandments, lying might not seem so bad. If you listen to Lucifer's line, then "love one another" can be twisted to cover up the clear command to "avoid sexual immorality" (1 Thessalonians 4:3).

When you refuse to pray "Your will be done," and have a spiritual temper tantrum in order to get your own way, you open the door to Satan. He'll offer several stimulating and sinful alternatives to the will of God. Your pride and arrogance can cause you to launch out in your own strength—and fail. Unless you humbly depend on God you'll never be an overcomer. Because "the One who is in you is greater than the one who is in the world," you *can* evade the devil's entanglements and stake your claim in *more-than-conqueror* country!

The principles of victory and peace aren't just some recipe from a self-improvement cookbook. They require prayer time in the presence of God—soaking up His Word to the point that obeying it becomes almost automatic, cultivating an intimacy with Him that inspires complete confidence, walking so closely with the Lord that you learn to depend totally on His power.

You're young and you have a chance to choose between being a crawling caterpillar Christian or a butterfly believer. Trying to live the Christian life in your own strength keeps you grounded. So many Christians begin by living in the Spirit, only to end up slugging it out with purely human resources. It's not meant to be that way. "For in the gospel a righteousness from God is revealed, *a righteousness that is by faith from first to last,* just as it is written: 'The righteous will live by faith' " (Romans 1:17, italics mine). Make your life a constant prayer, which by faith brings the risen Christ in to deal with every situation you encounter.

YOU HAVE AN APPOINTMENT WITH THE CREATOR OF THE UNIVERSE...

...to learn how to pray about life's specifics.

Learning to Pray in Temptation

DAY 1

Dear God, the temptation to _____ is so strong. I invite You to share this trial with me. You've said, "Never will I leave you; never will I forsake you" (Hebrews 13:5). I believe You. Thank You, Jesus, that You're with me even when I'm considering experimenting with drugs, even when I want to disobey my parents, even when I can't help but notice the pornographic decor of my neighbor's locker, or even when _____

_____.

Thank You that I don't have to fall into the devil's trap, no matter what, because I claim Your promise: "You, dear children, are from God and have overcome them, because the one who is in you is greater than the one who is in the world" (1 John 4:4). I acknowledge that You are all-powerful and will give me the victory over _____ if I surrender my every desire to You. Thank You that no matter what, You love me—that nothing needs to shock me or shake my faith. When I ask with the apostle Paul, "Who shall separate us from the love of Christ? Shall trouble or hardship or persecution or famine or nakedness or danger or sword" (Romans 8:35)—or peer pressure, or my failure, or the hectic pace of life, or _____? I can answer with him—"No, in all these things I am more than conqueror through Him who loved me" (Romans 8:37, *personalized*).

Lord, I know I can confidently obey You because You always have my best interests in mind. I know that Your rules were made not to keep me from having fun, but to protect me from harm. You have promised, "If you obey my commands, you will remain in my love, just as I have obeyed my Father's commands and remain in his love" (John 15:10). I know that Your love is unconditional and unchanging, and it's only my disobedience that puts clouds between me and the sunlight of Your love. I rely on Your power to overcome the temptation to _____
so that nothing will come between You and me.

Thank You, Lord, for the promises and information about temptation given in Your Word. When I'm tempted, I know I shouldn't blame it on You, because James 1:13 says, "For God cannot be tempted by evil, nor does he tempt anyone." My evil desire is the problem. The wrong desire behind the temptation to_____is

_____.

Lord, forgive me. I submit this desire to You.

When Satan tries to convince me that my case is special, that no one has been under such pressure before, and that sinning is my only option, I can claim Your words: "No temptation has seized me except what is common to humans. And God is faithful; he will not let me be tempted beyond what I can bear. But when I am tempted, he will also provide a way out so that I can stand up under it" (1 Corinthians 10:13, *personalized*). Lord, show me Your way out of this temptation.

Based on Romans 6:13, I will not offer the parts of my body to sin, as instruments of wickedness, but rather, I'll give the parts of my body to You as tools for doing Your will. My tongue is dedicated to building up, not to tearing down. My hands, instead of being lazy, will do all they can to help others. I dedicate my brain to thinking only thoughts that are pleasing to God. My sexuality is first to be protected and then to be enjoyed in accordance with Your holy plan. My eyes will look at things You approve of, and my ears will hear only that which glorifies You. (DON'T PRAY THIS UNLESS YOU MEAN IT.)

I choose to believe, with the apostle Paul, who said: "But thanks be to God that, though you used to be slaves to sin, you wholeheartedly obeyed the form of teaching to which you were entrusted. You have been set free from sin and have become slaves to righteousness" (Romans 6:17–18). I choose now to draw on your unlimited power to give me victory over _____,
and to become a slave to righteousness.

Learning to Pray When Someone Hurts You

DAY 2

Dear Lord, _____ said/did _____,
and it hurt me so much. Thank You that You understand how I feel, and You can heal broken hearts and repair damaged emotions.

I realize that if I keep thinking about this incident and allow bitterness to grow, I'll have a big problem on my hands. Instead, I'm determined to forgive _____, even if right now I don't think he/she deserves it. I receive from You the strength to obey Your command: "Be kind and compassionate to one another, forgiving each other, just as in Christ God forgave you" (Ephesians 4:32). Although You're perfect, You forgave all of my sin. As Your child, I should be like You and forgive _____, realizing that I often do wrong myself. I will to forgive, even though my emotions are putting up a terrible fuss and I feel like I can't forgive. I know You never give commands without supplying the strength to obey.

Lord, You even said, "Love your enemies, do good to those who hate you, bless those who curse you, pray for those who mistreat you"

94

(Luke 6:27–28). Give me love for _____. Take away all my resentment and bitterness. I pray that You will bless _____, and I promise not to go around bad-mouthing _____.

Every time the pain returns and the memory video replays in my mind, I determine to reaffirm my decision to receive God's resources of love and forgiveness. I won't go back on my word. Although my emotions may rage for a while, I know that sooner or later they will catch up with my will.

But, Lord, I still hurt. I thank You that You can do something about my damaged self-image and my shattered emotions. Thank You that You are the God who "heals the brokenhearted and binds up their wounds" (Psalm 147:3). Lord, right now my heart aches, and I ask You to heal it.

God, if there is some truth in what _____ said, and there is something I need to change in my life, show me what I need to do about it. If a mistake I made prompted this action, I ask You for forgiveness and the ability to change. As You direct me, I'm willing to make an apology for my part in this problem.

If these words/actions were greatly exaggerated or completely unwarranted, I refuse to let others define who I am, and I turn to You for a correct evaluation of myself. You loved me enough to send Jesus to die just for me. When others can do nothing but criticize, I can hear Your words of comfort: "I have loved you with an everlasting love; I have drawn you with loving-kindness. I will build you up again and you will be rebuilt" (Jeremiah 31:3–4).

When I don't measure up to the impossible standards others have set for me, I can meditate on who You are and how that affects me: "The Lord is compassionate and gracious, slow to anger, abounding in love. He does not treat us as our sins deserve or repay us according to our iniquities. For as high as the heavens are above the earth, so great is his love for those who fear him; as far as the east is from the west, so far has he removed our transgressions from us. As a father has compassion on his children, so the Lord has compassion on those who fear him; for he knows how we are formed, he remembers that we are dust" (Psalm 103:8, 10–14).

Knowing that You always love and accept me unconditionally, and that You are willing to forgive me soothes my hurting heart. All of this makes me want to love and praise You even more!

Learning to Pray When You Feel Like a Failure

DAY 3

Lord, how could I have done anything so dumb? Sometimes I feel as if I can't do *anything* right. But then, my mistakes confirm my theology. I know that I'm not a god or in the process of becoming one. I'm thankful that You don't expect me to be super-human, to have perfect judgment, or to have the wisdom of a Monday-morning quarterback! Thank You that You said, "As a father has compassion on his children, so the Lord has compassion on those who fear him; for he knows how we are formed, he remembers that we are dust" (Psalm 103:13–14). Thank You for accepting me and loving me in spite of my many problems and failures.

☑ If Your Failure Was Falling Into Sin

I know that _____
was a sin against You. I realize that "he who conceals his sins does not prosper, but whoever confesses them and renounces them finds mercy" (Proverbs 28:13). Thank You that "if I confess my sin, he is faithful and just and will forgive me my sin and purify me from all unrighteousness" (1 John 1:9, *personalized*). I confess _____

_____
as wrongdoing and make no excuses for my actions. I ask You for Your cleansing. I receive Your forgiveness and choose to believe You when You say, "I, even I, am he who blots out your transgressions, for my own sake, and remembers your sins no more" (Isaiah 43:25). I also pray, with David, "Restore to me the joy of your salvation" (Psalm 51:12).

☑ If Your Failure Involves Hurting Other People

Lord, I know (your action)_____
hurt (person) _____. You teach me that "if you are offering your gift at the altar [really participating in worship] and there remember that your brother [or sister] has something against you, leave your gift there in front of the altar. First go and be reconciled to [the person]; then come and offer your gift" (Matthew 5:23–24). I will

go to _____ and ask forgiveness for what I did. (WARNING!
DON'T PRAY THIS UNLESS YOU MEAN IT. BE SURE YOU KEEP
YOUR PROMISE TO GOD.)

Lord, I often feel ugly, clumsy, and socially inferior. Somehow
other kids manage to dress nicer, to be more popular, and to get better grades. I sometimes wonder, "What's wrong with me?" But when I
get these thoughts, I know I'm really falling into the *I'm-gonna-turn-
into-Wonder-Woman-or-Superman-or-bust* worldly thinking. I realize
that You explained in Your Word that we're all parts of the body of
Christ—with different gifts and different functions, and that all we
have or are is due to Your grace, so that bragging or comparing ourselves with others is ridiculous. Lord, help me to keep my eyes on Your
truth and to remember that jealousy is sin. It's also an indication that
I'm not satisfied with the way You made me and the place in Your kingdom You assigned to me.

Lord, I sometimes think of myself as a pretty lousy Christian.
Today I don't feel at all "spiritual" or "turned on" for Jesus. I do recall
that the devil loves to accuse Christians just to make them miserable.
I know that one major difference between the devil's accusations and
the Holy Spirit's conviction is that the Holy Spirit always pinpoints *specific sin*, while Satan comes down on us with a general *sense of failure*.

Since right now I don't know of any unconfessed sin in my life, I'll reject all these feelings of guilt that can't be pinned down and claim Romans 8:1–2: "Therefore, there is now no condemnation for those who are in Christ Jesus, because through Christ Jesus the law of the Spirit of life set me free from the law of sin and death." Thank You that Your purpose is to forgive me—not to condemn me.

I will be more concerned with what You think of me than with the things others have to say about me. *You* loved me so much You sent Jesus to die for me. *You* love me so much You're preparing a special place in heaven just for me. *You* love me so much I can say with David, "The Lord was my support. He brought me out into a spacious place; he rescued me because he delighted in me... It is God who arms me with strength and makes my way perfect. He makes my feet like the feet of a deer; he enables me to stand on the heights" (Psalm 18:18–19, 32–33). "The Lord will fulfill his purpose for me" (Psalm 138:8).

Thank You that You're responsible for making me a success, and that takes all the pressure off me. My part is simply trusting and obeying You. Lord, I submit every area of my life to You and determine not to worry about whether or not I measure up to the unrealistic standards and goals I have set for myself and others have imposed upon me. Instead of putting an *F* on my own report card, I'll let You grade me.

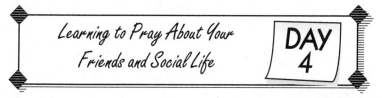

Learning to Pray About Your Friends and Social Life — DAY 4

Dear God, Your Word affirms, "Do not be misled: 'Bad company corrupts good character' " (1 Corinthians 15:33). But it's hard for me to find the right kind of friends. You know how it is at school. I often have to choose between eating lunch with kids who are a bad influence on me or sitting alone; between making fun of everything and everyone or sticking out like a sore thumb; between laughing at the dirty jokes in the locker room or becoming the subject of the next one. Thank You that You understand and that You're there to reassure me when I feel so totally out of it.

And I'll remember Your words and apply them to my life: "Happy is the kid who doesn't walk down the hall listening to the advice of non-Christians or stand by the lockers of students planning to sin, or sit at

McDonald's with those who do nothing but ridicule and mock others" (Psalm 1:1, *paraphrased*). If I obey, I know I'll be "like a tree planted by the streams of water, which yields its fruit in season and whose leaf does not wither. Then whatever I do will prosper" (Psalm 1:3, *personalized*).

Reminding myself of Your Word, I can realize that paying the high price of staying away from mostly pagan peers will be worth it in the end. Give me the strength to avoid bad company today.

Lord, You command me, "Let your light shine before men, that they may see your good deeds and praise your Father in heaven" (Matthew 5:16). You're not asking me never to associate with non-Christians, instead You're instructing me to be a testimony to them. You've told me, "But in your heart set apart Christ as Lord. Always be prepared to give an answer to everyone who asks you to give the reason for the hope you have. But do this with gentleness and respect" (1 Peter 3:15, *personalized*). I realize that the secret of being an influence instead of being influenced is to immediately identify myself as a Christian so that everyone around me expects me to live up to my convictions. Help me to always be willing to be different, and to let others know where I stand from day one. Keep me from the tremendous temptation to just fit in and flow with the group. Help me to always be able to see when the non-Christians around me stop listening to me and begin influencing my thinking. At that point, Lord, give me the courage to make myself scarce—even if it means being a loner for a while.

Lord, it's hard to stand alone. You've said, "Delight yourself in the Lord and he will give you the desires of your heart" (Psalm 37:4). I do want to fulfill the condition of this promise by making You Number One in my life—more important to me than popularity, than dates, than being accepted by the other kids. As I obey You at every turn, I ask You for Christian friends at school, in my neighborhood, and at church. Even some kids at church are very rebellious (though they fool a lot of adults), and hanging around with them would give me new temptations. Lord, give me friends who will lead me closer to God, not further away.

God, You know there aren't many Christian guys/girls to date. In spite of the fact that I realize it's wrong to date a nonbeliever, it's often very tempting. It's logical that if I'm not to "walk in the counsel of the wicked" or "be yoked together with unbelievers," I can't date a non-Christian. I don't have to tell You that. Dating means listening to a lot of advice and forming a yoke, or tie of sorts, which would obligate me to that person in terms of giving him/her my time, my loyalty, and my affection. Lord, for this reason, I want to date a person who loves You as much as I do.

Lord, I trust You to bring me the right Christian to date. You've promised, "I bestow favor and honor. No good thing do I withhold from you if your walk is blameless" (Psalm 84:11, *personalized*). If I'm living my life completely for You, I can be sure that the reason for being dateless is that right now You have something better for me or something to learn which will enrich my life. I can trust You to bring the right person into my life—at just the right time. Lord, I determine to "seek first his kingdom and his righteousness, knowing that Christian friends, fun times, social events, and dates will be given me as well" (Matthew 6:33, *paraphrased*).

Learning to Pray About Daily Details

DAY
5

Lord, I don't have any big problem to discuss with You today. But when I read Proverbs 30:17—"The eye that mocks a father, that scorns obedience to a mother, will be pecked out by the ravens of the valley, will be eaten by the vultures"—it scares me! Listening to the kids at school, I just assumed that rebelling against my parents was normal. Forgive me for making fun of their old-fashioned ways and trying to get out of the work assigned me. I've never even thought of applying Philippians 2:4—"Each of you should look not only to your own interests, but also to the interests of others"—to my parents! I rarely consider their needs, only my own.

Your Word says: "Honor your father and mother...that it may go well with you and that you may enjoy long life on the earth" (Ephesians 6:2–3). Help me to become more concerned about honoring them and obeying them than about standing up for my "rights." Only with Your help can I become less selfish. Only as You guide me can I turn into a better son/daughter. What changes do You have in mind for me? Give me a new idea for demonstrating the love I have for them.

You say: "Love is patient, love is kind. It does not envy, it does not boast, it is not proud. It is not rude, it is not self-seeking, it is not easily angered, it keeps no record of wrongs" (1 Corinthians 13:4–5). By Your

definition, I really don't love my brother/sister! Oh, God, forgive me for the bad attitudes I have toward my brother/sister. It always bugs me when he/she _____
(irritating or sinful behavior displayed). I haven't forgiven him/her for

_____.

I tell him/her I'm sick and tired of hearing "I'm sorry" over and over for the same offense, but I have an awfully long way to go to reach seventy times seven. Your command—"Do not let any unwholesome talk come out of your mouths, but only what is helpful for building others up according to their needs" (Ephesians 4:29)—is one I've never really applied to my brother/sister. I don't know when I last gave him/her an honest compliment. Lord, I'm sorry and I'm willing to apologize to _____. (DON'T PRAY THAT UNLESS YOU MEAN IT!) Teach me how to be a better brother/sister and give me a good idea for showing love to _____ today.

Then there's my bad attitude toward work around the house. You say, "And whatever you do, whether in word or deed, do it all in the name of the Lord Jesus, giving thanks to God the Father through him" (Colossians 3:17). Show me how to (your responsibilities around home)

_____,

_____,

_____,

in order to please You, and to do it with an attitude of thankfulness.

I've never thought of praying about keeping my room in order, but come to think of it, it's often a source of conflict between my mom and me. Instead of complaining to You that I wasn't born neat and

organized, I know I need to confess my laziness as sin and submit to Your training, a course taught by Your appointed teachers, my parents. I'm willing to go through the pain necessary to become a disciplined person. (DON'T PRAY THAT UNLESS YOU MEAN IT!)

My attitude toward school needs a complete overhaul. Although nobody likes _____ as a teacher, You've commanded me to love everybody—even my enemies. Lord, I will to receive Your compassion and understanding for _____, even if he/she is an unfair instructor. Instead of making fun of him/her, I will start praying for him/her. (DON'T MAKE A PROMISE YOU DON'T INTEND TO KEEP.) Paying attention during boring classes isn't easy either. Help me to remember that I'm going to school to glorify You and to learn all I can so You can better use me in the future. Your standard is: "Whatever your hand finds to do, do it with all your might" (Ecclesiastes 9:10). I certainly don't apply that to doing homework. Put Your values in me.

Lord, I'll no longer be satisfied with just getting through the day. Applying Your principles and praying about each detail of my life, I want each day to be a good and a godly day.

Note: These sample prayers and those in Chapter Two are designed to show you how to use relevant Scripture in order to pray about any situation. A concordance or a topical Bible (like Thompson's) will help you find the verses.

2

Just Between God and Me:
Parts of Prayer

Chapter Seven
Is "Thank You" Part of Your Vocabulary?

✔️ Putting the Thanks Into Thanksgiving

Crystal sat in chemistry class, not even trying to keep her mind on molecular structures. Neutrons and protons just couldn't draw her mind away from the perplexing personal problems that plagued her. Nothing could erase the past weeks' events from her mental video—and her haunting questions would not go away.

How could her father just announce that he had accepted a new position in Colorado where he was going to move in with his secretary? Why couldn't her dad realize how much this divorce was hurting everyone? And why couldn't her mother think of anyone but herself? As for her own personal life—why had Rick decided to break up with her and start dating Darla? Where was God in all this? Why did other kids seem so happy, while she was hardly able to cope? What would happen to her?

Although her parents argued a lot and her father had stopped going to church, Crystal had never dreamed that the problem was so serious. One Saturday morning at the breakfast table, her dad had dropped the bombshell: He was leaving in the afternoon. He assured Crystal and her older brother, Jack, that he loved them very much and hoped that they'd understand—but he was so much in love with Tanya that he just had to "follow his heart."

At that, Jack's anger had exploded. Now he could never even mention his father without resentment in his voice. Her mother had burst into sobs, and hadn't stopped crying since. Crystal had always been "Daddy's little girl." She had adored her father. Now the parent she had admired so much had let her down. The father who had always made sure that she dated "decent" guys and had told her never to lower her moral standards was now living with his flirting, mini-skirted secretary, even before his divorce was final!

Confusion, hurt, the feeling that maybe she could have prevented the problem mingled with rejection and depression.

Crystal had accepted Jesus as her Savior and thought she loved Him a whole lot—but now she was filled with fear and doubt. She couldn't concentrate enough to read her Bible. When she wasn't telling God the whole story for the 157th time, her prayers became pointed complaints. She even wondered if the Bible were true. What if everything she'd been taught all her life was wrong? Nothing was going right: Her grades were terrible, life was a drag, and she'd forgotten how to smile.

There seemed to be no one who really cared. At first, Rick had been understanding. Crystal really loved him and thought that with his help she could make it. But he had become disgusted with her. "You're no fun any more," he accused. "It's better that we break up." With that Rick had turned and walked out of her life, just like her father. At least her father and Tanya were in Colorado—Crystal had to watch Rick and Darla every day in the lunch line and pass them in the hall on the way to English class every day. The pain was so bad that her chest ached.

As chemistry class ended, Crystal realized that tomorrow would be Thanksgiving and she had nothing to be thankful for. Her mother had bought a turkey, and her grandma was flying in from Cleveland. But how could they celebrate without her father? Thinking of Christmas was even worse. Her father had already sent her tickets to come to Colorado during vacation. He promised skiing in the mountains, meals in fancy restaurants, and a tour of Denver. But traveling all that way alone just to watch her father lavish his attention on the secretary Crystal had never liked anyway seemed more like torture than holiday happiness.

Somehow she got through the school day and walked home. Entering the big empty house just reinforced her desperation and loneliness. In a minute the doorbell rang. It was Kaari, a single woman from her church whom she hardly knew. In Kaari's hands was a gorgeous bouquet of chrysanthemums.

"I brought you flowers," she began, "because I know what it's like to face the first holiday after your parents separate. My parents divorced when I was in high school, and I still remember how awful it was. Our church is big and I'm not the kind of person who is up on all the news. If I'd known before, I'd have visited you long ago."

Tears welled up in Crystal's eyes. "Thank you," she said. "I'm having such a hard time I just don't know what to do."

Kaari set the flowers on the table and put her arms around Crystal. "I understand," she offered. "I've been there. Your emotions won't help you to make sense out of anything now. But you can trust God to work out even the ugly things caused by the sins of others to His glory and your good.

"When my parents broke up," Kaari continued, "I was devastated for months. I doubted my salvation and I thought God was unfair. But slowly I began to see that God's love was still there, and that He still had a meaningful plan for my life. I learned to depend solely on Him because there was no one else. I came to understand that my reason for living was Jesus and that no one could do anything terrible enough to interfere with the flow of love, joy, and peace that comes from Him. God has also used my suffering to enable me to empathize with others and to help them."

Crystal had admired Kaari for a long time. She was cheerful and kindhearted. The fact that she was unusually beautiful, musically talented, and had worked her way into a top job while still in her twenties—without losing her humble touch—all of it impressed Crystal. She had assumed that Kaari had no problems whatsoever.

"Both of my parents have remarried," Kaari went on. "And because of problems in each marriage, I've lost my home. Neither Mom nor Dad has invited me for the holidays. But I've volunteered to serve the Thanksgiving meal at the rescue mission, and I invited a couple people to come to my place afterward."

As they talked about a lot of other things, Crystal realized how much Kaari cared for her. "Crystal," Kaari offered as she was leaving, "I want to be your friend. I want to help you through this difficult time. Here's my phone number. You can call me anytime—day or night."

After Kaari left, Crystal picked up the family cat and sat down on the sofa to have a little talk with God.

"Lord," she confided, "I do have something to be thankful for. Thank you for Kaari." That genuine prayer of thanks felt so good she added, "And thanks that Grandma will be here, that we're in a country where we can enjoy the luxury of a big turkey dinner—and that Calico always purrs when I pet her."

YOU HAVE AN APPOINTMENT WITH THE CREATOR OF THE UNIVERSE...

...to learn how to tell Him thank you.

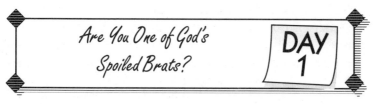

A radio speaker affirmed that he had made a vow to thank God every day for sending Jesus to die on the cross and to save him from hell. "To my knowledge," he continued, "I've never broken that promise." How often do you say thank you for your salvation?

"Christ left heaven to be born in a manger—to experience hunger, pain, and rejection so you and I could receive eternal life. He shed his blood for you. Although He was God and could have called 10,000 angels to rescue Him, He voluntarily endured the beating, the verbal abuse, the crown of thorns, the nails, and an excruciatingly painful death just for you. You're saved by grace through faith alone—you don't have to do anything because Jesus did it all." You've probably heard these awesome things so often that the miracle of Calvary and the incredible gift of full forgiveness for sin no longer impresses you.

But the heart of Jesus that was pierced for you deserves to hear your expression of gratitude. The nail-scarred hands wait for your offerings of thanksgiving.

The hardness and casualness that take salvation for granted and forget to thank God for His grace are very dangerous. The writer of Hebrews asks a penetrating question. "How shall we escape if we ignore such a great salvation?" The Greek word translated *ignore* has the following meanings: to make light of, neglect, and not regard. Forgetting to constantly thank God for saving us makes us guilty of taking such a great salvation for granted.

Are you one of God's spoiled brats whose thoughts are so filled with pepperoni pizza, impressing members of the opposite sex, buying the right clothes, having fun, and being popular at school that there's no space left for appreciating what Jesus did for you on the cross? Maybe you should make it a point to thank God every day for freedom from guilt, a purpose for living, and the hope of heaven, remembering that none of these things would be yours if Jesus hadn't died for you!

Steps TO TAKE

1. Process Impressive Information

Giving thanks to the Father, who has qualified you to share in the inheritance of the saints in the kingdom of light. For he has rescued us from the dominion of darkness and brought us into the kingdom of the Son he loves, in whom we have redemption, the forgiveness of sins. (Colossians 1:12–14)

May I never boast except in the cross of our Lord Jesus Christ, through which the world has been crucified to me, and I to the world. (Galatians 6:14)

Therefore, if anyone is in Christ, he is a new creation; the old has gone, the new has come! All this is from God, who reconciled us (made us His friends) to himself and gave us the ministry of reconciliation. (2 Corinthians 5:17–18)

Give thanks to the Lord, call on his name; make known among the nations what he has done. (Psalm 105:1)

2. Consider Radical Response

Dear God: Forgive me for sometimes thinking of my salvation as no big deal. Help me to consider what it would be like to be "without hope and without God in the world." Thank You for sending Jesus to suffer and to shed His blood so that my sins could be forgiven. Thank You for letting me hear the gospel and for saving me. Help me to never forget to express my gratitude.

3. Listen Before Proceeding

Wait before God in silence, receiving His changes in your attitude.

4. Prepare for Action Application

Read Matthew 26:20–75 and Matthew 27:1–50, stopping to say thank you for each thing Jesus went through to gain salvation for you.

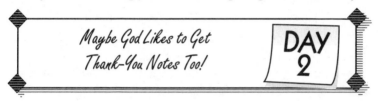

Maybe God Likes to Get Thank-You Notes Too! — DAY 2

For weeks, Neil's family had prayed for his mom's health. When the doctor discovered that she was taking the wrong medicine and corrected the error, she improved dramatically. Neil, who was then a junior in high school, made a statement I'll never forget: "We prayed and prayed that God would heal my mother—and now I'm determined that we'll spend equal time thanking Him."

How much time do you spend expressing your gratitude to God when He answers one of your petitions? Do you remember to say thank you? Or do you have a never-ending list of requests while you routinely acknowledge all that God has given you with a childish, "Lord, thank you for everything"?

It's easy to think that the mighty God who created the universe doesn't need to hear you say "thank you," but that's not true. God commands us to thank Him, and the Old Testament prescribed sacrifices of thanksgiving. It troubled Jesus that nine of the ten lepers He healed didn't even bother to return to express their appreciation. Don't you think that the God who sent His Son to die for you—who loves you unconditionally, and who "richly provides us with everything

for our enjoyment"—is saddened by your ingratitude?

Not only should you say thank you, but your thanks, like your petitions, should be specific: "Lord, thank You for helping me get an A in history; thank You for giving me the Christian friend I prayed for; and thank You that I made the basketball team."

You really shouldn't ask God for anything without also thanking Him. "Do not be anxious about anything, but in everything, by prayer and petition, with thanksgiving, present your requests to God" (Philippians 4:6). How about deciding to invest the same amount of time thanking God for His answers to prayer as you spent asking?

Steps TO TAKE

1. Process Impressive Information

I thank and praise you, O God of my fathers: You have given me wisdom and power, you have made known to me what we asked of you, you have made known to us the dream of the king." (Daniel 2:23) (Daniel did not forget to thank God for answered prayer!)

Three times a day he got down on his knees and prayed, giving thanks to his God, just as he had done before. (Daniel 6:10) (Part of the secret of the powerful praying of Daniel was that he thanked God daily!)

At the dedication of the wall of Jerusalem, the Levites [those who served God in the temple] ...were brought to Jerusalem to celebrate joyfully the dedication with songs to thanksgiving and with the music of cymbals, harps, and lyres [small stringed instruments]. (Nehemiah 12:27). (It is important to express your gratitude to God for each accomplishment in your life.)

Save us, O Lord our God, and gather us from the nations, that we may give thanks to your holy name and glory in your praise. (Psalm 106:47)

...he will continue to deliver us as you help us by your prayers. Then many will give thanks on our behalf for the gracious favor granted us in answer to the prayers of many. (2 Corinthians 1:10–11) (Prayer and thanksgiving go together.)

2. Consider Radical Response

Dear God: Thank You for always listening to me. Thank You for answering me when I prayed for _____ and _____.
Forgive me for ingratitude and help me always to say "thank You" when You answer my prayers.

3. Listen Before Proceeding

Be still before God so that the lesson from His Word that He wants to teach you today can sink in.

4. Prepare for Action Application

Write God a thank-you note expressing appreciation for answers to prayer and for things you've received from Him without even asking for them.

Is Thanksgiving the Missing Ingredient in Your Prayers?

DAY 3

If you break your ankle the day before you plan to leave on a summer missionary outreach trip, should you thank God for the broken ankle and all the good that will come from it? Or should you thank your all-powerful God that He is in control of each circumstance and ask Him to heal your ankle so you can go?

It seems to me that your prayer should be subject to discerning God's will in the specific situation. But one thing I know—you should be thankful. "Always giving thanks to God the Father for everything in the name of our Lord Jesus Christ" (Ephesians 5:20) gives us no loopholes for complaining or for temper-tantrum prayers that demand our own way or refuse to wait for God's timing. Scripture directs us to have grateful hearts.

A fish out of water, a junior-high boy at a formal dinner for retired ladies, or a grandmother dressed like a teenager are somehow very out of place—and therefore miserable. So is an ungrateful person. In contrast, when you thank God you're doing what you were made to do and you feel good. The person whose heart is always filled with gratitude is happy and well-adjusted. We're not made to second-guess God, and lack of thankful confidence in His ways can lead to ulcers, frustration, sleeplessness, tension headaches, and many other undesirable by-products. Nothing steals our joy like refusing to be thankful.

Is the missing ingredient in your prayer *thanksgiving*? Have you been praying for a boyfriend or girlfriend without thanking God for the friends you have right now? Do you plead with God to change your parents without expressing gratitude for all their good points? When you ask God to use you, is there more resentment for the talents you lack than thanksgiving for the abilities God has entrusted to you?

Learning to say *thank you* is a first step in learning to pray because it acknowledges dependence on a sovereign God who knows what He is doing. There will be times when you don't understand what is happening and when you don't even know how to pray, but even then you can always obey the clear command, "Always giving thanks to God the Father for everything."

Steps TO TAKE

1. Process Impressive Information

For although they knew God they neither glorified him as God nor gave thanks to him, but their thinking became futile and their foolish hearts were darkened. (Romans 1:21)

Let the peace of Christ rule in your hearts, since as members of one body you were called to peace. And be thankful. Let the word of Christ dwell in you richly as you teach and admonish one another with all wisdom, and as you sing psalms, hymns and spiritual songs with gratitude in your hearts to God. And whatever you do, whether in word or deed, do it all in the name of the Lord Jesus, giving thanks to God the Father through him. (Colossians 3:15–17)

Give thanks in all circumstances, for this is God's will for you in Christ Jesus. (1 Thessalonians 5:18)

2. Consider Radical Response

Dear God: I realize that I was made to thank You and can see how ingratitude makes me into a crabby person. I've been complaining about _____,

_____,

and _____.

Instead, I want to thank You for _____,

_____,

and _____.

Thank You that You're smart enough to give me what's best. Help me to express my gratitude to You even when I don't understand.

3. Listen Before Proceeding

In a moment of silence let God speak to you.

4. Prepare for Action Application

Try a five-minute thanksgiving prayer. Time yourself. Pray out loud if possible—and thank God for everything you can think of. If you find yourself lacking for things, start over again. This may be harder than you think—maybe you need practice in thanking God and should do it every day!

Have You Thanked God for the Person You Just Can't Stand?

DAY 4

Have you ever thanked God for the leaders of your country, the teacher who makes your life miserable, or the kid whose snide remarks erode your self-confidence? If you haven't, you're disobeying a scriptural command: "I urge, then, first of all, that requests, prayers, intercession, *and thanksgiving be made for everyone*" (1 Timothy 2:1, italics mine). We are to thank God for all the people in our lives.

Studying what the Bible has to say about thanksgiving, I was surprised to find that the apostle Paul was constantly giving thanks to God for the people he ministered to. He even begins his letter to the Corinthians with "I always thank God for you"—and those dudes were really messed up. Friction, immorality, law suits, disorder, and pride within the church were only some of the problems. I would have probably started Corinthians with "I'm totally disgusted with you all."

Paul tells the Thessalonians: "But we ought always to thank God for you"—and that included at least a few freeloaders who refused to work for a living. When Paul began his defense before Felix, acknowledging his reforms "with profound gratitude," I believe he could say this because he had thanked God for Felix in his prayers. Part of the secret to Paul's unusually successful ministry was the greatness of his gratitude.

Some very positive things occur when we start thanking God for people. Gratitude delivers us from the victim's syndrome and enables us to see God's greater purpose in allowing difficult people to affect our lives. It's possible to thank God for the atheist mayor and at the same time see that he was placed in power to wake up Christians enough to organize for the next election. You can give God thanks for the insensitive gym teacher and the crabby boss who helped you come to terms with the fact that you must please God, not people. Expressing gratitude for people also forces you to find the good in them. And as you start to thank God for everyone, you begin to change your attitudes.

Thanking God for a person before you pray that God will change him or her is good strategy. Thank Him for your parents, your teachers, your principals, your church leaders, your boss, and even for the police—it will help you to respect authority. If you forget to be thankful, your prayers can disintegrate into gripe sessions in which you share with God all the latest gossip. If you're truly grateful for those around you, the day will come when you can honestly say to another, "I thank God for you!"

Steps TO TAKE

1. Process Impressive Information

I thank my God every time I remember you. (Philippians 1:3)

And we also thank God continually because, when you received the word of God, which you heard from us, you accepted it not as the word of men, but as it actually is, the word of God, which is at work in you who believe. (1 Thessalonians 2:13)

I always thank my God as I remember you in my prayers. (Philemon 4)

First, I thank my God through Jesus Christ for all of you, because your faith is being reported all over the world. (Romans 1:8)

2. Consider Radical Response

Dear God: Thank You for the people You've placed in my life—thank You for my parents, my relatives, my friends, my pastor, and my church. Thank You for my classmates and my teachers. And thank You for those who are giving me difficulty right now: _____, _____, _____ and _____. Help me to see Your purpose in bringing each of them into my life. (But don't forget that it is *your* responsibility not to choose non-Christians as your best friends.)

3. Listen Before Proceeding

Wait in silence for any thoughts God might want to give you.

4. Prepare for Action Application

Make a list of the authorities in your life and the difficult people you must deal with. Spend time every day this week thanking God for these people. After your time of thanksgiving, you may pray that God will change them!

Practicing Thanksgiving **DAY 5**

Have you ever sunk the winning basket, answered the question that stumped everyone else, fixed the sound system so the show could go on, won a contest, baked the cake that everybody raved about, or worn the coolest T-shirt? If you have, just remembering the event gives you satisfaction and renewed self-confidence. Reliving past victories can be a valuable tool in helping us face today's challenges.

Gratefully recalling all the wonderful things God has done for you—what I call "thanksgiving thinking"—can really build your faith. As you remember how God came through in the past, you will more easily be able to commit your problems to Him in prayer.

Several psalms follow the *God-was-faithful-in-the-past-trust-Him-for-the-future* format. I used to laugh when I read Psalm 136. I thought that making such a big deal about thanking God for making the sun, drowning Pharaoh in the Red Sea, and putting an end to Og, King of Basham, was just a little weird. I don't anymore. I should thank God that the Bill of Rights was added to the Constitution, that my great-grandfather was a dedicated Christian, and that my parents always sent me to Bible camp. It makes me realize that God engineered every detail to place me here for a very specific purpose.

Remembering how God used an atheist to pave the way for me to teach a Bible and archeology course in public high school, how He caused my friend to say, "Lorraine, why don't you write a book?"—the exact words I'd prayed that someone would tell me if I was to really try such a thing; and answered our intercession for fellow faculty members by allowing me to help lead a teacher who had once been a Communist to Christ encourage me to ask God for other things. Try thanking God for all that He has done in your life.

Not only should you thank God for granting your requests, you ought to form the habit of thanking Him for the sunlight, for new shoes, for your biology book (it would be a treasure in some countries!), for your mother's smile, for the fact that you don't have a cold, and for the chance to play volleyball with your friends. The formation of "thanksgiving thinking" requires training. While walking home from school, cleaning your room, or waiting for the last bell to ring, decide to turn your thoughts toward the things God has done for you and thank Him once again. Practicing thanksgiving will yield big dividends.

Steps TO TAKE

1. Process Impressive Information

Enter his gates with thanksgiving and his courts with praise; give thanks to him and praise his name. (Psalm 100:4)

Let them sacrifice thank offerings and tell of his works with songs of joy. (Psalm 107:22)

"But I, with a song of thanksgiving, will sacrifice to you." (Jonah 2:9)

Give thanks to the Lord, call on his name; make known among the nations what he has done. (1 Chronicles 16:8)

We give thanks to you, O God, we give thanks, for your Name is near; men tell of your wonderful deeds. (Psalm 75:1)

2. Consider Radical Response

Dear God: I want to make thankfulness a habit. I've never thanked You for _____, _____ and _____ but I'm thanking You now. And I forgot—I also want to thank You for _____, _____ and _____.

3. Listen Before Proceeding

In silence let God remind you of other reasons to give Him thanks.

4. Prepare for Action Application

Make a long list of things you've never thanked God for and spend time thanking God. (It might help you to pretend that you had lived in a poverty-stricken village in India and were suddenly transported to your present surroundings. Through those eyes you see a lot to be grateful for.)

Chapter Eight
When 911 Prayers Just Won't Do the Job

Instead of experiencing the anticipation and excitement that a new school year usually brought, Josh found that his first day as a senior at Park High filled him with fear. It suddenly hit him that within nine short months the security of his pre-programmed existence was about to end. He would have to face the tough decisions that were to affect the rest of his life. Where should he go to college? What should he spend at least a big part of the rest of his life doing?

His problem was that there were too many options. An honor-roll student who had lettered in both basketball and baseball, he had been told by his counselor that he'd be in line for several scholarships. His coach thought he had a chance to play professional baseball. His mom, a missionary's daughter, hoped he would attend the Bible college that she and his grandfather had graduated from—regardless of other offers. Josh was totally confused. He enjoyed science a lot and at times pictured himself as the doctor who not only attended to the physical needs of his patients but pointed them to faith in God. Of course, he imagined himself pitching for the Minnesota Twins, but at other times he wanted to be a missionary to South America like his grandfather.

He was panicked enough about the future to check out some books from the church library on listening to God and finding God's will. He read something that convicted him: "Guidance does not come from an empty mind; it comes to a heart full of the love of Jesus Christ. If day by day I will turn to my Bible and honestly and earnestly seek to find God's will, He has guaranteed to show it to me: His Word is a light to my path and a lamp unto my feet. This process will take discipline! It will take time. It will mean that you are going to turn to the Bible every day. Nothing in your day—any day—must be allowed to crowd out that quiet time spent on your knees with your Bible and prayer."[1]

Josh knew he should be having daily devotions, but he just never got around to it. Because he was a serious student and accustomed to rigid athletic training, he never expected that setting aside ten minutes each morning to read his Bible and pray would be so hard. But he decided to plug away at it.

The first thing that really convicted him had little to do with going to college. As he read "Love the Lord your God with all your heart and

---

[1]Alan Redpath, *Getting to Know the Will of God* (Chicago: InterVarsity Christian Fellowship, 1954), p. 15.

with all your soul and with all your mind and with all your strength"
(Mark 12:30), he realized that his girlfriend Winona was preventing
him from doing that. Although she attended his church and professed
to be a Christian, her commitment was very shallow. Never even considering the element of God's will in the situation, she was strongly
urging him to attend the local state college where she would be studying. Her values were materialistic and selfish, and more often than not,
he just went along with her.

But she was incredibly charming, unusually beautiful, and full of
fun. Wherever she went she attracted admirers, and he was the envy
of all the guys when he brought her to school events. Besides, she was
really in love with him, and he thought he loved her.

A couple things he read really jolted him out of his complacency.
"The whole issue on the question of guidance is this: if you want to
know God's will for your life, *are you prepared to pay the price of knowing it?*"[2] That price is absolute surrender to God on *every* issue. There
is no shortcut. "Don't expect God to reveal His will for you next week
until you practice it for today."[3]

He knew he'd have to give up Winona if he were to find God's will
for his life. For weeks he struggled. Would he really surrender his life
to Jesus to do whatever He wanted? Right now it meant breaking up
with Winona, but later on it might mean changing his comfortable
lifestyle to become a missionary or forfeiting the popularity he loved
so much to take a politically incorrect stand based on the values he
believed in.

Finally one night when a special speaker gave a sermon on the
high cost and great rewards of totally following Jesus, Josh knew he
had to go forward to make that commitment to 100-percent
Christianity. As he drove Winona home, he explained to her that God
was asking him to break off their relationship. She didn't understand
and began sobbing uncontrollably. When that didn't work, she angrily
accused him of having ulterior motives, slammed the car door, and
ran up the sidewalk to her front door. His heart ached and he longed
to calm her down and put his arm around her shoulder just once
more. Only the words of the sermon that played again and again in his
mind kept him from running after her. "When obeying God is the
hardest thing you've ever done in your life never take back the deci-

[2]Ibid., p. 8.
[3]Ibid., pp. 17–18.

sion." That time was now and he had to remain firm.

Trying to make Josh jealous, Winona immediately started dating Jim. It was hard to see them together, but he knew he couldn't waver. One evening his mom confided, "I've been praying for three months that you'd break up with Winona. She's beautiful, but she would have kept you from God's best."

"Thanks, Mom," Josh replied. "I know you're right." Although his emotions put up a terrible fuss, his mind told him he could never follow God completely if he chose to marry a woman like Winona.

But Josh wasn't getting any closer to making a decision about college. The Bible said nothing about higher education, and he couldn't even find principles he thought applied to his situation. He tried the things he found in one of the books. He made lists of pros and cons for all his alternatives, but the lists were of equal length. He asked the advice of his pastor, his youth leader, his father, his mother, and his grandmother. All of them told him the same thing. "None of these options is bad and each could be used for God's glory. You have to follow the guidance the Holy Spirit is giving *you*."

He reread the booklet on decision making. It stated that if Scripture, the inner confirmation of the Holy Spirit, and circumstances (less important and not always reliable) coincided, a Christian could determine that God was leading him in a certain direction.

Obviously, the key in his situation was learning to recognize that inner voice of the Spirit. One book maintained that the kind of prayer twentieth-century Christians knew nothing about was *listening* prayer. "A conversation," wrote the author, "has two parts: talking and listening. We're always so busy detailing all our problems that we never stop to consider what God is telling us. Hearing God requires both time and silence—the two scarcest commodities in modern culture."

Then he read a book that recommended setting aside whole 30-minute time slots just to listen to God. The writer maintained that it was like having a date with God to get to know Him on a much more personal and intimate basis—clearing away the mental clutter and getting out of the rat race long enough to really hear His voice. He found some steps for doing just that:

1. Slowly read a passage of Scripture, pausing to reflect on each thought.
2. Sit in complete silence, entrusting each worry and fear to God.

Sense His protection, His care, and His loving arms around you.

3. Realize that you're in the presence of a holy God. Yet He who is all-powerful, all-knowing, and everywhere-present is also the One who loves you unconditionally.

4. Surrender each selfish desire, each stubborn rebellion, each bad attitude to the Lord. Renounce any thought or action that is contrary to His will.

5. Open yourself to let God show you if there's something in your life that makes it impossible for you to hear His voice. Sin has to be dealt with before you can have clear communication with God. "Your iniquities have separated you from your God; your sins have hidden his face from you" (Isaiah 59:2).

6. If God shows you that something is wrong in your life, confess it as sin and ask His forgiveness. (Remember that the Lord forgives sin—not excuses.) Hate that evil action or thought and do everything possible to never get involved in a rerun. Really receive God's complete forgiveness. God says He "remembers your sins no more" (Isaiah 43:25). You'd do well to imitate His attitude!

7. Concentrate on God and His attributes—love, justice, kindness, holiness, power, etc.

8. Listen for that still small voice of the Holy Spirit within. Be willing to obey what God tells you to do.

9. Praise Him and thank Him.[4]

This really sounded different to Josh, because he only knew how to pray "give-me prayers," but he really wanted to give it a try. When his sister and parents left for the weekend, he went into the family room to spend that silent time with God. He felt awkward at first, but after a while he sensed the wonderful warmth of God's presence—and a couple of changes the Lord wanted to make in his attitudes. However, he sure didn't know any more about where to go to college.

Later, a statement he read assured him that he was on the right track: "The whole question of guidance is not our relationship to the particular problem, but our relationship to the Lord Jesus Christ,"[5] Josh did want to get to know the Lord so well that he would be able to hear His voice. He found other half-hour time slots to spend before the Lord in silence. They were times of special closeness to God.

[4]Most of the basic ideas in this outline are borrowed from Joyce Huggett, *Listening to God* (London: Hodder and Stoughton, 1986), pp. 54-73.
[5]Alan Redpath, *Getting to Know God* (Chicago: InterVarsity Christian Fellowship, 1954), p. 6.

One night at the supper table, his mother said something that at first startled him. "I got a phone call from my friend Bernice in California," she began. "She doesn't know what to do with Christi. She likes to lock herself in her room for hours and says she's listening to God. She now claims that she has received revelation that the world will end on March 17. She wants to quit school because she figures it's a waste of time."

Josh hadn't told anyone about his quiet times with God—but now wondered if he was off on some dangerous tangent. He hadn't yet finished the book on listening to God, and he doubted it would be in his church library if it contained dangerous teaching. The next chapter did a lot to clear things up for him. Because of passages such as Jude 3, which speaks of "the faith that was once for all entrusted to the saints," it was obvious that God was not about to reveal any new doctrine to anybody. The author put it like this: "Listening to God is not about the *newness*, but about *nowness*. It is receiving the applied word in whatever form God chooses to make it known."[6] A further explanation stated that every thought came from one of three sources: God, your own mind, or the evil one—Satan himself.

By applying certain tests one can discover whether or not the idea really came from God:

1. Is it completely in line with Scripture?
2. Is my attitude humble and Christlike?
3. Does it prompt me to live in a way that honors God and obeys Him?
4. Do two other mature Christians also feel that it is God who is leading me to take this course of action?
5. Do my spiritual leaders approve of my action? (If a group has become totally disfunctional and non-biblical, this would not apply.)
6. In cases in which the Spirit of God prompts you to do little things like call a friend at a certain moment, break off a certain friendship, or sign up for a different English class, you can't and shouldn't continually consult other Christians. Trust God to confirm that He was really speaking, by the circumstance itself: Your friend will say, "I really needed a phone call tonight"; the kid you stopped hanging around with will get into some trouble; or you'll find out that

[6]Joyce Huggett, *Listening to God* (London: Hodder and Stoughton, 1986), p. 91.

the class you transferred out of is very poorly taught.[7]

If Christi were using these tests, Josh thought, *she would immediate-ly realize that her prediction and anticipated action were not from God.*

Josh then discovered a little book called *The Practice of the Presence of God* written by Brother Lawrence, a seventeenth-century monk who worked as a cook. He believed "our only business" is to "love and delight ourselves in God." He disciplined himself to keep his mind on Jesus even when his silence was disturbed by the clatter of pots and pans and by the bickering of the other kitchen staff. Josh had never even thought of developing thought patterns that would teach him to turn his mind consciously toward God when it was not needed to solve a trig problem, figure out how to pitch to the lead-off batter with bases loaded, or get his car to start on a cold winter morning. He thought that if he could concentrate enough to make free throws even when the crowd was going bananas, he could learn to think about God during his day. He decided that bringing God's presence constantly to his consciousness was worth the mental fight. He knew he'd have to begin small, and not try to compete with Brother Lawrence. He decid-ed to write out some Bible verses about the character of God on three-by-five cards and stick them in his pocket. During the five minutes before the bell rang each period, he'd slip a card into his book and med-itate on it. When he walked to and from school, he'd sing praise songs and turn his mind toward God.

During the first week of using his new strategy, his mind was harder to control than their German shepherd dog—who felt that his freedom should not be restrained by any leash. He was glad to read that even those who were experts at concentrating on God were plagued by stray thoughts. Even though his mind jumped from con-templating the greatness of God to surfing on a California beach, and from thanking his Maker to wondering if the physics test would be multiple-choice this time, and even to things less innocent, he also found that consciously making an effort to think about God at the end of each period made his school day a lot easier.

Josh continued his three-pronged approach. He read his Bible and prayed every morning. He tried for a half hour of silence before God each week, and determined to refocus his mind on God (using the Bible

---

[7]These points are taken from Joyce Huggett's book *Listening to God* and an article by Leonard Le Sourd, "What Is God Saying to You?"

verse cards whenever possible) at the end of each class hour and walking to and from school.

When spring came, he received attractive offers from three universities and a chance to sign for a major league farm club. Instead of the previous fear, he had peace. He developed a sense of conviction that the option he felt drawn to was God's leading in his life. He subjected that guidance from the inner voice of the Holy Spirit to the opinions of his parents and trusted Christian friends. After spending a half hour in stillness before God with the specific prayer—"Lord show me if I'm wrong," he still felt the same peace. One morning he read Isaiah 30:21: "Whether you turn to the right or to the left, your ears will hear a voice behind you, saying, 'This is the way: walk in it.' " That verse seemed like his final confirmation. God had not used anyone to give him solid Christian advice against the plans he was about to make. He didn't sense any stoplights along the way. God had been faithful to reveal His will.

Josh realized he'd have a lot more decisions to make in his life—in fact, Diana, the new pastor's daughter, promised to be one of them. Not only would he have to maintain his ways of keeping in touch with God, he'd need to expand and refine them.

Finding God's will for your life can't happen through emergency praying. It happens as you open lines of communication with God through daily contact in prayer.

YOU HAVE AN APPOINTMENT WITH THE CREATOR OF THE UNIVERSE...

...to learn strategies for getting to know God better.

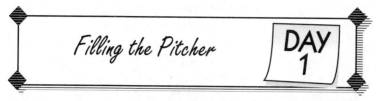

Filling the Pitcher DAY 1

Andrew Murray once said, "Selfishness is the death of prayer." And so it is. But no one would argue that a young mother of four who insists on taking care of her own health is on an ego trip. After all, if she gets sick, her children will suffer. A teacher who takes a year off for further study is not accused of neglecting the students. The missionary doctor who is so busy attending patients that he can take no time to consult his medical books in difficult cases is not a model humanitarian. Selflessness in prayer doesn't mean only praying for the needs of others. If you don't receive spiritual life from God each day, you'll have nothing to give.

On the other hand, prayer can degenerate into a pity-party, a lust for emotional thrills, a self-centered exercise, or a daily list of wants handed to "the Great Santa Claus in the Sky." Because of the big emphasis today on service and praying for others—very important elements in the life of the spiritually healthy person!—burn-out is a widespread problem. We need to maintain a balance—receiving from God in order to give out effectively to others. And to achieve this balance, we need to concentrate on establishing or strengthening our devotional lives.

The fact is that you must constantly return to God for refills of *love-your-enemy* love, encouragement to persevere when the going gets tough, and power to resist the torrents of temptation that come your way. Without the still small voice of God's guidance, you'll make unwise decisions that will complicate your life and rob you of God's best. Unless you're thoroughly acquainted with biblical principles, you'll never be able to give godly advice. The stress and anxiety of life will do you in if you don't learn how to retreat into God's presence where all is peace and love and genuine joy.

Actually taking the time to "sit at the feet of Jesus," basking in His love, reflecting on His words, and waiting for Him to impress ideas on your spirit is the most unselfish thing you can do, for it will greatly increase the quality of service you can render to others. But it is also of utmost importance for you personally. When you bow before the all-powerful God, who loves you unconditionally, to get His perspective, mountains become little hills, and "I can't " changes to "I can do everything through him who gives me strength" (Philippians 4:13).

Even if you spend all Saturday catching up on sleep and doing what you most enjoy, there is a part of you that still hasn't been refreshed. Your spirit needs to touch God's Spirit. Your mind needs to be renewed. The world's ideas of constant competition, necessity to be noticed, and accumulating more stuff, must be replaced with God's goal for your life—humbly obeying Him and serving Him while enjoying the sweetness of His presence. This has to be a daily affair because we so easily slip into making shopping an obsession, having to prove ourselves to someone, or just following the crowd. We so often forget that our citizenship is in heaven—unless we make frequent phone calls to the city where the streets are paved with gold.

Not only does quiet time with God build us up to refresh others, our Lord himself desires fellowship with us. "Here I am! I stand at the door and knock. If anyone hears my voice and opens the door, I will come in and eat with him, and he with me" (Revelation 3:20).

We can't earn our salvation, and our spending time with Him isn't for the purpose of chalking up brownie points. But one of the few things we can do to thank God for all He's done for us is to give Him our love. And as we love and adore Him, we fulfill a deep need within us to give and receive love. Romance stories don't end with, "He told her once that he loved her and never mentioned the matter again." Love must be expressed over and over. Your entering a daily love relationship with Jesus—the only One who'll never disappoint you or take advantage of your affection, the One who'll never leave you or forsake you, and the One who's preparing a place for you in heaven—is the best investment of time and energy you'll ever make.

And if you constantly refill your pitcher, the "empty glasses" you meet can receive from you the love and joy and encouragement of Jesus.

Steps TO TAKE

1. After each thought presented in Joshua 1:5–9, pause to listen to God. Then write down the way in which God is applying it to your particular present situation. If there is no specific application, leave the space blank.

"No one will be able to stand against you all the days of your life."_____

_____.

"As I was with Moses, so I will be with you." _____

_____.

"I will never leave you nor forsake you."_____

_____.

"Be strong and courageous, because you will lead these people to inherit the land I swore to their forefathers to give them." _____

_____.

"Be strong and very courageous." _____

_____.

"Be careful to obey all the law my servant Moses gave you."_____

_____

_____ .

"Do not turn from it to the right or to the left, that you may be successful wherever you go." _____

_____.

"Do not let this Book of the Law depart from your mouth." _____

_____.

"Meditate on it [God's Word] day and night, so that you may be careful to do everything written in it." _____

_____.

"Then you will be prosperous and successful." _____

_____.

"Have I not commanded you? Be strong and courageous." _____

_____.

"Do not be terrified; do not be discouraged." _____

_____.

"For the Lord your God will be with you wherever you go." _____

_____.

2. Decide how to put into practice the insight you've received.

3. Follow the same format with the following passages: First write out the phrase, then be still, waiting for God to show you something special He wants *you* to know. Write that down. If you have to skip some phrases that's okay.

Matthew 6:25–34
Philippians 4:4–9
Romans 12:9–18
Colossians 3:1–10
Hebrews 12:5–11
Galatians 6:1–10

Turn Your Radio On   DAY 2

God is God, and He can illumine your mind with His thoughts while you're ringing up a sale, or memorizing the forms of a French verb, or talking back to your mother! But if you tune in to His frequency, you're much more likely to hear from Him.

In fast-paced and media-oriented modern life, a half hour of silence is a miracle. There are a lot of demands on your time and mental concentration that aren't optional—school, work, church activities, social life, and maybe sports, rehearsals, baby-sitting, jobs around the house, etc. Obviously, recommendations like "pray constantly," and "Be still and know that I am God" don't mean *consciously* turning your thoughts to God all day long every day. It is impossible to meditate on Scripture while you're quarterbacking a football game, following the band director through a hard piece of music, or trying to remember all the things the boss told you to do before closing time! You can't intercede for each person on your prayer list during the biology exam. But you can learn to maintain an attitude of companionship with God, returning your thoughts to Him whenever your mind is free to wander.

This takes practice. During the activities that don't require much brain-drain, you can train your mind to pray or to think about God. Most likely your parents taught you to pray before you eat. That habit is so automatic that at least three times a day you thank the Lord—and if you're like me, those 30 seconds of conversation with God have helped you through some pretty hard days. You can develop other strategies for turning your thoughts heavenward.

Falling asleep each night meditating on a verse of Scripture, thanking God, or reflecting on His faithfulness can save you from insomnia, temptation, and fear. Just try mentally repeating one biblical thought over and over again as you drift off to sleep. If you're like most people, you need a rather short phrase like, "He is my fortress, I will never be shaken," or, "I am with you always," or, "Do not worry about tomorrow," because your brain is exhausted at that point and can't be expected to work very hard. That simple exercise can keep you from dreading taking the driver's test, imagining that a special someone crawled into bed with you, or planning revenge on the kid who teased you so unmercifully.

Waking up each morning repeating, "This is the day the Lord has made; let us rejoice and be glad in it," or saying, "Good morning, Lord, thank you for my home, my health, my clothes, my family, my school, and my dog," can beat the devil to the punch. Satan is so good at inserting wrong thoughts into our minds and then accusing us of having thought them. If you don't habitually turn your mind toward God the minute your alarm rings, then thoughts like, "It's raining and I don't want to get out of bed," "Giving that science report will be horrible, so maybe I should just skip school," or, "I can't stand to face another boring day," are sure to come to you.

In case you haven't noticed, some of the devil's most ferocious attacks come when you haven't quite awakened yet, or when you're just falling asleep so your mind isn't alert enough to be on the defensive. You need a good offense for the beginning and ending of your day.

If you invest in some good praise songs and other uplifting Christian music, your Walkman can help you out. Get rid of any cassettes or CDs that won't bring you closer to the Lord, and listen to music that will place your thoughts on God.

How about putting something inside your locker to remind you of God's love? Every time you open it, take a moment to remember that God loves you—no matter what happened last hour, even if you lost your math assignment, and regardless of the fact that your friend purposely ignored you when you passed her in the hall. Forming the habit of thinking of God's great love for you and thanking Him for it every time you open your locker at school could change a lot of your days.

Going running or walking in the conscious companionship of Jesus is a neat experience. You can share your joy, your failure, your disappointment, your fear, your anticipation, your insecurity, your excitement, or your heartbreak with Him. When your mind wanders—and it will—gently refocus it on Christ. If a computer were to capture your inner dialogue, the printout would read something like this: "Lord, that tree is really awesome. You did a great job of designing it. You know, I'm not sure about signing up for art next year. What do *you* think? You have my future planned, and I need your advice. My mom's been really crabby lately. Am I doing something wrong? Give me a good idea for making her happy today. Forgive me for snapping at my sister. I know you want me to apologize, but I've been putting it off. Okay. I give in. I'll do it. Help me study for the history test tomorrow."

Taking a Bible-verse card along to center your thoughts, spending part of the time singing hymns, or using the last three or four minutes just to quietly listen to God might prove helpful.

Actually, you can turn your negative thoughts or statements into times to practice the presence of God. It's kind of like putting on the whole

armor of God and quarterbacking plays that defeat the devil's offense.

When "how could I be so dumb?" escapes from your lips, reaffirm "Lord, thank you that you love me just the way I am." If you're about to say, "What a lousy day," decide to thank God for the rain. Instead of joining all your friends in making fun of Mr. Green, pray for him. Complaining about lunchroom food could be replaced with gratefulness that you get something to eat. The "I can't stand him" turns into "Lord, help him. He's got a lot of problems."

"It's not fair that all the other kids have the newest running shoes and I don't" becomes "God, I thank you that during this time when my father is out of work I can love my family and love You."

As you plan with God, He'll give you other ideas for practicing His presence daily. Remember that one of the strongest deterrents to bad habits is establishing good ones. Sure, sometimes praying before each meal, or saying "Thank you, Lord, for the day" each morning can become merely routine. But it's surprising how often God breaks into that established pattern with His special love and light. So many times I have felt God's presence fill a dreary, droopy day with His brightness just because I paused to consciously invite Him to share that moment with me. Turn your mental radio on and tune in to God. Your life will be richer for it.

Steps TO TAKE

1. Select one or two of the ideas presented, or come up with one of your own to consciously form the habit of turning your thoughts toward God.

2. Take a whole month to establish this thought pattern in your brain. For each day, rate your progress, G = Good, F = Fair, P = Poor, and on a weekly basis record how this new habit helped you.

EXAMPLE

S	M	T	W	T	F	S
1	2	3	4	5	6	7
G	F	P	F	G	P	G

Thursday morning I started the day by thanking God for everything I could think of. Instead of the usual mad rush to catch the bus, I had peace as I got ready and actually got to the bus stop early.

This Month I'll Practice the Presence of God by working on these two strategies:

1. _____
   _____

2. _____
   _____

Grade yourself good (G), fair (F), or poor (P) for each day and write out the account of your victories:

S	M	T	W	T	F	S

_____
_____
_____

_____

S	M	T	W	T	F	S

_____
_____
_____

_____

S	M	T	W	T	F	S

_____
_____
_____

_____

S	M	T	W	T	F	S

_____
_____
_____

_____

S	M	T	W	T	F	S

_____
_____
_____

_____

A Leash for Your Hyperactive Imagination

DAY 3

Erin began praying that her school friend Mallory would give her heart to Jesus. "Lord," she pleaded, "do something to open her eyes so she'll see that knowing you is more important than always having the right clothes."

But at that point, Erin pictured the awesome jacket Mallory had just purchased, and her mind immediately jumped to the one she'd seen at Nordstroms. It was perfect. If she saved the next two paychecks, she could buy it, and she knew she'd get a lot of compliments. Suddenly, Erin realized how materialistic *she* was. She felt like a hypocrite who couldn't even concentrate for two minutes to pray, and she wondered if it was any use to continue asking God to reach Mallory....

Garret decided he'd pray for ten minutes and that he'd time it. He started praising God and thanking Him for specific things. He continued, "Thank you, Lord, for the victory over Kennedy High." At that moment, his quarterback mind started constructing the perfect play to be executed against Robert E. Lee on Friday night. Their defense had been severely weakened when their best end had suffered a bad injury. His play would take advantage of the defective pass defense. Abruptly he remembered that he was supposed to be *praying*—not winning a

...Dear Lord... Bless Kevin!...

football game! He just mumbled: "I guess I can't pray very well. Amen." Garret didn't like to fail, and it was just easier to exit.

Matt's prayer was even worse. When He thanked God for the blood of Jesus, it brought back scenes from the movie he'd watched the night before. It even crossed his mind that he ought to learn some of the violent moves he'd seen to make Spike—the guy who harassed him mercilessly—shut up. Once the sequence of violent events was replayed mentally, Matt was horrified. "If I can think about hurting someone like that," he mused, "I must not even be a Christian."

Do you identify with any of these scenes? Do you have a terrible time concentrating in prayer? You might be comforted to know that even great men and women of God face the same problem. Keeping your mind on praying isn't easy! But the conquering of inner space—and that will change your world—is a most worthy goal. Decide to accept the challenge.

📝 The Necessary Info

1. *The devil is trying to sabotage your prayer time, but you have the power of Jesus to stop him.*

Satan is capable of inserting thoughts into your brain and then accusing you of having thought them! He acts just like an armed robber who, seeing a policeman, thrusts the gun into the hands of his victim, shouting, "Look, he's trying to shoot me!" The devil robs you of your communication with God by interjecting a terrible thought into your mind and then whispering, "You're a terrible Christian. Anyone capable of thinking that must not even be saved!" *Don't let the enemy pull this on you!*

Being tempted isn't sin, and you're not responsible for the evil thoughts that invade your praise time. But you could sin by following up those evil thoughts with some reasoning of your own. Or you can call the devil's bluff! You can calmly and with authority say, "In the name of Jesus beat it!" Then go back to your praying as though nothing had happened. Be sure to put this strategy into operation.

2. *By constant practice you can learn to concentrate better and better.*

Parents don't spank the twelve-month-old baby who falls while learning to walk, and God doesn't condemn inexperienced prayer warriors for their inability to concentrate. He will react with delight because you've decided to learn how to communicate with Him—no matter how much your mind wanders. Don't expect praying to be easy. It isn't.

3. *Some planning will help you.*

Have a pencil and paper ready. If you suddenly remember "I didn't finish the math assignment," or, "I forgot to call Chris," or, "I have to bring my parent permission slip back today," you can just write it down and go on praying.

Treat a straying thought or a full-fledged fantasy like a little kid that appears in the middle of the basketball court during the game— gently remove it and go on. The devil's purpose is distraction. If he can make you bemoan your failure or get upset about your daydreaming or wandering thoughts, he's got you. Simply return to praying so you lose a minimum amount of time.

Pray out loud in order to concentrate better.

Change activities whenever you get bogged down. Read the Bible instead of praying. Sing a praise song out loud if you're falling asleep reading Leviticus, etc.

Focus your thoughts by writing a letter to God.

Decide to discipline your mind in every area. That will help you pray better. Learn how to really study. Listen in class instead of day-dreaming. Take notes on sermons. Keep your mind on a tight leash!

The more you practice concentrating in prayer, the better you'll become. You learn to pray by praying. Stick with it and don't give up.

1. Read a psalm, personalizing it and praying it out loud—that means putting it into your own words, maybe modernizing the concepts, and using first-person pronouns (I, me, and my). Have a pencil and note pad ready for writing down something you must remember to do, and the minute you realize your mind is wandering, gently bring it back to the task at hand. If you can't concentrate enough to do this spontaneously, write it out first. The following is an example.

Psalm 91—God Will Protect Me

I can constantly live under Your protection and You're my all-powerful God. However, if I stray far from Your safety zone and _____

_____

(sin I'm tempted to commit) only to scurry back when I see imminent danger, the insurance policy You promise doesn't automatically cover me. However, if I stay by Your side I can relax, even if_____

_____

because You're so near I feel as if I'm in Your shadow.

I'm telling You, Lord, You're my bomb shelter, my bullet-proof vest, my car alarm system, *and* my personal policeman, so I trust You to shield me from the storms of life. You will save me from the trap set for me by _____, who enjoys seeing Christians like me fall, and from the plague of _____ that's going around our school right now.

Thank You that I can feel safe in You, just like a chick under its mother's feathers. I'll find refuge in You when _____

_____ .

Your faithfulness will be my air cover, my tank, and my Patriot-Missile system. I won't be afraid of the street violence at night, or of the gangs who invade my school in broad daylight, or of getting held up, or of innocently contracting AIDS because of a medical slipup. I won't fear _____, _____ or _____ because You're there watching out for me.

A thousand might get so depressed they will never rise again, and ten thousand may be utterly wiped out—but I'm indestructible, because if something happens to my physical body I'll just exchange it for one that no one can ever hurt again. If I follow You wholeheartedly, I'll only be an observer to the punishment of the wicked.

As I make my permanent home with You, deciding never to leave, You will always be my refuge. Staying right with You, I can claim that no harm will come to me and disaster won't stop at my house. Lord, You'll command angels to guard me when _____

_____

_____ .

_____

and_____

are problems for me. Angels will carry me so I won't stumble over the rocks and boulders of sin, false ideas, and wrong decisions. Through You, Jesus, I can be victorious over the devil—that old lion who is looking for someone to eat up, that snake who keeps on inventing Eve-like temptations.

Lord, I do love You with all my heart. Make my love so pure that You will say, "I will rescue you." Thank You that "the name of the Lord is a strong tower; the righteous run to it and are safe" (Proverbs 18:10). I acknowledge Your name and receive Your protection.

I will pray to You and expect Your answer. I claim Your promise, so I know that You will be with me in trouble to deliver me and honor me. Thank You that You'll stuff a lot of living into my life-span and constantly demonstrate Your saving power.

2. Now be still before the Lord and let Him speak to you.

3. Using the same system, personalize and pray the following:
Psalm 103—God's love letter to you.

Psalms 63, 64—God's promise to you when others unfairly attack your reputation or try to harm you.

Psalms 12–16—God's promise when it seems that evil and corruption have taken the upper hand.

Psalm 101—Taking a stand on personal conduct and the friends you choose.

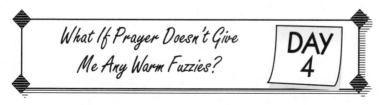

What If Prayer Doesn't Give Me Any Warm Fuzzies? **DAY 4**

In my surveys and conversations with high school kids, what do you think the students identify as the number one problem in their prayer lives? *Consistency.* Nothing else even came close.

The world runs on a *if-it-feels-good-do-it* philosophy, implying you shouldn't engage in any activity that doesn't give you immediate self-gratification. So the answer I got is not surprising. Self-discipline has become an old-fashioned word—along with spinning wheel, covered wagon, and juke box. The Bible talks a great deal about self-discipline, though, and you can't become a committed Christian without it. The *power* comes from God, but we must cooperate with Him or it will never flow through us. "Work out your salvation with fear and trembling, for it is God who works in you to will and to act according to his good purpose" (Philippians 2:12–13). An automobile engine has all the power, but it's still work to drive a car—especially in heavy traffic. You must depend on God for power and directions, but He has assigned certain responsibilities to you.

The Bible commands us to pray. "Pray continually" (1 Thessalonians 5:17). "And pray in the Spirit on all occasions with all kinds of prayers and requests. With this in mind, be alert, and always keep on praying for all the saints" (Ephesians 6:18). "Then Jesus told his disciples a parable to show them that they should always pray and not give up" (Luke 18:1). If you are not praying, you are not obeying God!

Steps TO TAKE

In prayer you learn to communicate with God and develop a relationship with Him. Building a relationship takes time, energy, and commitment. Effective communication requires your best effort. A cutting-edge prayer life will require the following:

1. *Renew your love and commitment to Jesus.*

Do you really love Him enough to sacrifice something for Him? Will you obey Him even if it costs you an awfully lot? Do you really intend to give up other things that are important to you so He can have first place in your life? If you can't answer *yes* to each of these questions, you might as well not read on—the other points won't help you unless your commitment is firm. (However, you *can* repent and then take the quiz over again!)

2. *Rearrange your schedule so that you give your best time to God in prayer.*

1 Peter 4:7 lays it on us: "Therefore be clear minded and self-controlled so that you can pray." If you're so exhausted you can't see straight, you can't pray. If you have so many things going you're a basket case, you can't pray. One of the most important requirements for a consistent prayer life is getting enough sleep so you can be alert for prayer. It means getting to bed at a decent hour—often retiring

before you know who won the game or giving up going out with your friends. (Sometimes, arranging your own transportation so you can leave early will solve the problem.)

In order to spend priority time in prayer, you'll have to take something else out of your schedule. Here are some options:

- Learn to spend less money and work fewer hours.
- Watch a lot less TV.
- Give up an extracurricular activity at school.
- Give up some of your social life and devote the time to prayer.
- Write out how you spend every hour for a whole week and bring it to an efficient person who is a committed Christian. Let him or her give you pointers on how you can eliminate wasted time so you can pray more.
- If you're a compulsive studier, addicted to top grades, study less and pray more.

You can't just squeeze prayer time into an overcrowded schedule; you'll have to sacrifice. Ask God what you'll have to eliminate in order to have an effective prayer life.

3. *Decide to pray—even when you don't feel like it.*

Although God often allows us to feel His presence and at times sense a certain inner joy in prayer, there are other days when we feel *nothing.* Never check your emotional temperature. Just start praying—no matter what. God will bless that consistency.

4. *Expect prayer to be hard work.*

It's easier to switch on the TV, read a comic book, or call a friend than it is to pray. Your body would rather go swimming, take a nap, or eat pizza than pray!

Prayer takes heavy concentration. It's necessary to constantly resist the devil who is doing everything possible to keep you from praying. Use some sanctified creativity to fight Satan's efforts to keep you from praying effectively. If you're tired and find yourself turning into a couch potato, do some exercises without interrupting your conversation with God. You can pray for your school while doing sit-ups! Splash some cold water in your face and walk around as you ask God to improve your relationship with your parents. Pray out loud so you don't drift into daydreaming. Use a list of things to pray for so you don't lose your focus.

5. *Realize that most results of prayer occur in the invisible spiritual world.*

Some teens get discouraged because they don't *see* immediate answers. Your prayers are kind of like the bombing of Pacific islands during World War II before the Marines stormed the beaches. Although no one saw exactly what happened in those "softening up" maneuvers, that paved the way for victory. Keep praying that you'll overcome your addiction, that you'll learn how to communicate with your father, and that you'll be able to share your faith without fear. Something *is* happening behind the scenes. Obey God and wait for visible results.

6. *Try praying for ten minutes straight.*

Praise God, thank Him, confess your sin, pray for others and for situations. Then pray for yourself. This will seem like a long time at first, but you'll get used to it.

A Helpful Habit   DAY 5

Let's face it, sometimes you have no creativity or imagination. You need a comfortable mold for your quiet time, a familiar routine. Although this book gives you many ideas to use during your devotions, you need a format you can always go back to. *A guide to time with God each day,* which follows, is just that. I'd suggest you make a copy, back it with cardboard, and keep it by your Bible. When you don't know what else to do during devotions, follow this outline. It will help you to maximize your time with God.

Steps TO TAKE

☞ A Guide to Time With God Each Day

1. Begin by thanking God for the privilege of having a personal appointment with the Creator of the universe, and ask Him to show you new things from His Word and teach you to pray better.

2. Read a praise psalm as a prayer of thanksgiving, substituting *I* and *me* for the pronouns you, him, etc., to make it personal. (Praise Psalms: 9, 19, 27, 34, 46–48, 92–93, 97–98, 100, 104–105, 107, 111, 113, 115, 121, 135, 138, 144–150.)

3. Read a chapter in the Bible. (I recommend starting with the Gospel of Mark.)[1]

   a. Read the chapter twice.
   b. Choose a title for the chapter that describes the general theme.[2]
   c. Write down any examples to follow or actions to avoid.
   d. Jot down your questions about any hard-to-understand passages, and bring them to your youth worker or pastor to answer for you at a later time.
   e. Listen to God as you read the passage. Write down the thoughts the Holy Spirit brings to your mind while meditating on this chapter.
   f. Copy the commands in this chapter. Write out the changes you have to make in your life in order to put them into practice.
   g. If you wish, write out a paragraph summary of the chapter.

4. Take time to pray.

   a. Praise God for who He is, remembering His characteristics—like all-powerful, loving, all-knowing, etc. You could make up a little song to sing to Him or use a hymn or praise song you know.
   b. Sit quietly, receiving God's love and enjoying the fact that He is your friend.

---

[1] It would be great to decide to read the same chapters as a good friend, to be accountable to each other for following this guide each day, and to talk over what you're learning. (This could be dynamite in a dating relationship.)

[2] It's a good idea to use a notebook. And it would be helpful to make yourself accountable by showing your notebook to someone—parent, pastor, or friend.

c. Thank God for everything—material blessings, physical health, opportunities to grow spiritually, the chance to get an education, and what you will learn from the problems you're facing.

d. Confess and forsake any sin in your life. Follow through on making things right. (For example, after you ask for forgiveness for yelling at your mother, apologize to her.)

e. Pray for your family, friends, school, church, community, country, people you know who haven't accepted Jesus, missionaries, world situations, and your own life.

f. Give God your life, your actions, and your thoughts for this day.

g. End by thanking and praising God again.

Chapter Nine
Pizza With Bill, Irregular Verbs, and Spring Break

▶ Confess It and Forget It

Chelsea was a straight-A student—in fact, the counselor had just called her into his office to inform her that she was tied with Ryan Adams for top scholastic honors. After four years of hard work, she had a chance to be valedictorian of the senior class. She was overjoyed—and scared to death.

Ryan was a brain who had almost no study habits—and didn't really need them, considering the classes he'd chosen. Chelsea had some of the same instructors, so she knew they were easy graders. Her problem was third-year Spanish. Miss Rivera was ready to retire, and her method of teaching was definitely old-fashioned. She seemed to delight in torturing her students. Her sadistic weapon was irregular verbs, which had to be memorized in present, imperfect, preterite, future, and conditional tenses. Her predictable tests called for one verb form after another.

Chelsea spent hours learning verb forms—she even dreamed she discovered a secret machine that would come up with any verb in the desired tense if she pushed a button.

Miss Rivera decided to give a unit test Friday before spring break. It couldn't have come at a worse time. Because Chelsea had picked up some rare virus, she missed four days of school. Barely recuperated, she had only a week to pack and arrange everything to leave at 5:00 A.M. Saturday morning with the youth mission team to spend their vacation in Mexico. There just wasn't much time to study. Thursday night, Bill called and invited her to Pizza Hut—and she'd been dying to go out with him for six months. They spent a great evening together.

But once she closed the door to her room that night, a feeling of panic swept over her. She wasn't ready for the Spanish test first hour. If she stayed up all night to study, she might get sick again and not be able to go to Mexico with Bill and the other kids. Yet, if she didn't do something, she'd miss her chance to become valedictorian. Overwhelmed and exhausted, she remembered how Marissa laughed at her for studying, declaring that crib sheets worked just fine. She couldn't—she was a Christian. But a voice seemed to whisper from the shadows made by the lamp at her desk: "Miss Rivera is an unfair teacher, and just this once you're justified. Make the sheets. It's good review for you, and tomorrow you can decide whether or not to use them." So Chelsea copied the verbs in tiny letters on little sheets of paper.

The next morning she faced a civil war within. She reasoned that if all the other kids cheated, making the curve impossible, she had no choice. She'd just carry the answers in her pocket and perhaps it wouldn't be necessary to use them. She took her assigned seat in the back corner of the room. The exam was the usual—filling in blanks with irregular verbs. She answered the whole test, finding that there were five answers she questioned. Her conscience reminded her that she had once cheated in the fifth grade and it had turned out to be a disaster. But Miss Rivera was sitting at her desk reading a book, and the girl in front of her was brazenly copying from a full sheet of paper. It would be so easy and no one would ever know. Her hands were sweaty and her mouth was dry. Her hand was shaking but she reached into her pocket and silently pulled out the papers. Chelsea was so organized that in two minutes she had changed three answers and assured herself of a perfect test score. When the bell rang she gave a sigh of relief and handed her test to Miss Rivera.

The next morning she got up at 3:30 A.M. to do her hair just right and make sure she didn't forget to put everything in her suitcase. Bill had saved a seat for her, excitement was in the air, and she was about to make her dream visit to Mexico—but all Chelsea could think about was a crib sheet and three irregular verbs.

Once she got to Tijuana it was even worse. Every time she tried to communicate in Spanish, an irregular verb would enter the conversation. When they prayed together, Chelsea felt as if God were light-years away. They painted a church, showed the kids at the orphanage how to play with the games and the toys the group had brought, and put on skits in the parks, after which the Mexican kids shared their faith with whomever happened to be around. Chelsea participated in everything, but her heart just wasn't in it. "I think you're still not over that infection," Bill worried. "You seem to lack a little of your spark."

Their second morning in Mexico, the youth pastor led in devotions. "I had a different talk planned," he began, "but I think the Lord wants me to talk on confession of sin. Proverbs 28:13 reads, 'He who conceals his sins does not prosper, but whoever confesses and renounces them finds mercy.' I think you all remember the story of Achan. Because he disobeyed God by stealing some silver and gold and fashionable clothing, all of Israel was defeated at Ai. Those of us here who have unconfessed sin in our hearts will not feel bold for the Lord and so, in a way, the ministry of the entire team will be hindered. I want all of us to be silent for a few moments and to get right with God."

Chelsea began to cry. She forgot her excuses and told God, "I was wrong. Please forgive me for cheating on that test."

The youth pastor's wife, Cherie, came up to her afterward and asked if she'd like to talk. Chelsea told her the whole story. Cherie listened attentively before speaking. "Chelsea," she instructed, "you'll never have peace until you tell Miss Rivera what you've done and face the consequences. Although you usually shouldn't confess a sin to anyone who's not directly concerned, in this case it would be good if you told the whole group. You see, you were chosen for a team of ten out of the whole youth group and you were sent by the church to this short-term missionary project. Unconfessed sin affects the ministry of the entire team."

Chelsea swallowed her pride and did one of the hardest things she'd done in her whole life—she told the group what she'd done. Encouraged by her example, one of the guys confessed resentment against the youth pastor and asked for forgiveness. After that, two girls who had trouble getting along confessed the jealousy and competition they struggled with.

All of them sensed the presence of God as never before. Chelsea felt as though she'd just been released from prison. That afternoon their skits in the park were different. There was unity and commitment in what they did and people seemed drawn to them in a special way. Bill's comment surprised her, "Chelsea, it took a lot of courage for you to be honest before the whole group. I admire you for what you did."

A horrible thought crossed Chelsea's mind. What if she'd just kept covering her tracks without confessing? She had come so close to just stuffing her sin under a pretense of faithfulness and good deeds. She had almost opted for a life of misery and hypocrisy.

YOU HAVE AN APPOINTMENT WITH THE CREATOR OF THE UNIVERSE...
...to learn more about confession and forgiveness.

The Price Tag of Forgiveness — DAY 1

"It doesn't matter what you do, God will always forgive."

"If God pardons me for doing a whole bunch of bad things I'll have a more interesting testimony."

Have you ever heard or thought anything like this? A lot of people just take forgiveness for granted because they forget that it's a wonderful miracle that cost God a lot.

Just put yourself in the place of someone who has never heard the truth about the forgiveness Jesus offers us. Imagine the anxiety and frustration of being told that you can never be sure if you've made the grade or not, that you must perform certain good deeds or rituals to try to please some distant higher power, and that everything depends on *your* achievement. What would it be like to live with an underlying sense of guilt that won't go away? How stressful it would be to always wonder whether you've done enough. Aren't you glad that you know that "the blood of Jesus, his Son, purifies us from all sin"? Aren't you thankful that you heard the good news that Jesus paid the full price for all your sins so that you're saved by faith and not by works? But do you really appreciate how much your forgiveness cost God?

J. Edwin Orr explained that there are two principles of forgiveness: (1) Someone must pay the penalty. (2) The one who forgives suffers. For instance, if I lend you $1000 and I forgive your debt, I suffer the loss. If your father bails you out, he pays a price.

Jesus took the punishment for your sin, and that sin caused Him great physical and mental suffering. Don't ever take forgiveness for granted. There's no excuse for rattling off the thoughtless *and-Lord-forgive-all-my-sins-amen* prayers with the same lack of reverence with which you'd recite "Peter Piper picked a peck of pickled peppers!" Every sin is lethal. When you ask for forgiveness, appreciate that this great miracle is available to you only at a tremendous cost. Confess your sin, receive God's forgiveness, and then thank God for this priceless gift.

It's easy to think, "Sure Jesus suffered to provide me forgiveness, but that was two thousand years ago. It's all over now." I'd like to suggest that His forgiving you still costs Him a lot.

Steps TO TAKE

1. *Read Luke 15:11–32.*
2. Now reread it, putting yourself in the place of the father and answering the following questions:

    a. How do you feel when your son comes up to you and says, "Hey, Dad, I can't wait until you die for my share of the inheritance—I want it now"? _____

    b. What emotions do you experience when your son moves to a foreign country? _____

c. How do you respond when you don't hear from your son for months at a time? _____

d. What is it like to see your son coming in the distance? _____

e. How do you react when your son says he's sinned and deserves punishment? _____

f. What emotions do you struggle with when your older son becomes angry and refuses to attend the party? _____

g. How do you feel when your older son shows his jealousy, accusing you of not even letting him invite his friends over, but throwing a big party for his kid brother who has ruined the family reputation?_____

h. What did it cost you to forgive the younger son? _____

i. What did it cost you to forgive the older? _____

j. Returning to the present, what new insights did you receive about the price of God's forgiveness as you read this passage?_____

What Really Happens When You Confess Your Sins?

DAY 2

You've probably heard this somewhere: "When you repent of (admit and turn from) your sins, receive forgiveness, and invite Jesus to take control of your life, all of your sins—past, present, and future—are canceled out." Confession of sins is necessary to experience "new birth"—the supernatural miracle of becoming a totally different person in Christ. Let's look at how the Bible describes what takes place: "I, even I, am he who blots out your transgressions, for my own sake, and remembers your sins no more" (Isaiah 43:25). "Therefore, if anyone is in Christ, he is a new creation; the old has gone, the new has come!" (2 Corinthians 5:17). "I tell you the truth, whoever hears my word and believes him who sent me has eternal life and will not be condemned; he has crossed over from death to life" (John 5:24).

Salvation is our position in Christ—we've admitted that we can't save ourselves, have totally committed our lives to Him, and have confessed our sins to receive forgiveness and eternal life.

Salvation in no way depends on our own efforts—only on our willingness to permit Jesus to save us. A drowning man cannot save himself, but he has two choices: (1) He can splash around and fight like crazy, refusing to give the lifeguard a chance to help him; or (2) He can give up and let himself be rescued. Like the drowning man, you can be saved only by recognizing that you are helpless.

"If my sins are all taken care of and I'm on my way to heaven," some people ask, "why is it necessary to confess them as I commit them?"

This illustration may help you. It's reasonable to assume that a loving mother will forgive her child no matter what he has done. However, all of us know from experience that if that kid breaks his mother's prettiest vase while playing basketball in the house and tries to hide the evidence, he'll feel uncomfortable around his mother. Although there's forgiveness in her heart, the mother will react when she finds a few pieces of the broken vase. Only admitting the truth and asking for forgiveness will restore his *relationship* with his mother. We must confess every sin because sin keeps us from a clear communication with God and destroys our fellowship with Him.

Sin in our lives makes real prayer impossible: "If I had cherished sin in my heart, the Lord would not have listened" (Psalm 66:18). "Surely the arm of the Lord is not too short to save, nor his ear too dull to hear. But your iniquities have separated you from your God; your sins have hidden his face from you, so that he will not hear" (Isaiah 59:1–2).

Although a Christian who keeps totally depending on Jesus is free from the *necessity* of sinning, when he or she does sin, only admitting and confessing that wrongdoing makes it possible to be rightly related to God and to other believers. First John—which contains phrases like, "You dear children are from God," and is obviously written to Christians—gives us a full explanation of the reason a Christian must confess his or her sin. "If we walk in the light, as he is in the light, we have fellowship with one another, and the blood of Jesus, his Son, purifies us from all sin. If we claim to be without sin, we deceive ourselves and the truth is not in us. If we confess our sins, he is faithful and just and will forgive us our sins and purify us from all unrighteousness. If we claim we have not sinned, we make him out to be a liar and his word has no place in our lives. My dear children, I write this to you so that you will not sin. But if anybody does sin, we have one who speaks to the Father in our defense—Jesus Christ the Righteous One. He is the atoning sacrifice for our sins" (1 John 1:7–10; 2:1–2). We cannot have fellowship—a clean and beautiful communication with God—unless we agree to admit before God any behavior that does not line up with Scripture.

Now, it is true that a Christian does not have to sin. When Jesus died on the cross, the *power* of sin was broken. If we've truly decided that He will be the boss of our lives and receive *His* power to obey His commandments, we will experience victory over sin. However, we can also make the unnecessary choice to do our own thing and decide to sin. Sometimes ignorance of God's Word causes us to unintentionally disobey Him. In either case, the moment we realize we've sinned, we must agree with God that we have done wrong and ask for forgiveness.

Because the devil's chief delight is making Christians feel like strangers to God, causing them to question His love, and giving them a blah and boring outlook on life, he fights for all he's worth to keep you from confessing your sin. Rationalization is a Satan-assisted art. Even a little kid can come up with a dozen reasons to justify his wrongdoing. Admitting that you are wrong is terribly difficult—right?

But confession of sin is a wonderful privilege. It's the method God has designed to restore all the joy of having an intimate friendship with Jesus after we've blown it by treating Jesus like dirt. Actually it all boils down to this: A constant willingness to confess sin results in freedom and joy, while refusing to agree with God that we've sinned leads to frustration, depression, and defeat.

Pride is our great enemy. It tells us that since you didn't act any different from everyone else, you must not have done anything that terrible. And it constantly asks, "What will other people think?" My intentions were okay, so it doesn't matter what I did—is another cop-out. Don't let pride rob you of the peace with God that comes from squarely admitting your sin. Confession of sin is a wonderful privilege and that's why it's part of the pattern prayer Jesus gave His disciples: "Forgive us our debts, as we also have forgiven our debtors" (Matthew 6:12).

Steps TO TAKE

1. Memorize Proverbs 28:13—"He who conceals his sins does not prosper, but whoever confesses and renounces them finds mercy."

2. Ask God to show you any unconfessed sin in your life. Be totally honest with Him. Admit where you've done something the Bible says is wrong, and ask the Lord to forgive you.

3. Review this verse every day this week, repeating it again and again. Only "overkill memorization" will insure that you will remember the verse for the rest of your life—and this is a verse you'll need often. Trust me!

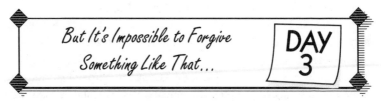

But It's Impossible to Forgive Something Like That... **DAY 3**

"I can never forgive him for what he's done to me." Have you ever heard that or said it yourself? Do the biblical commands to forgive seem unfair to you? How do you feel when you read verses like this?— "For if you forgive men when they sin against you, your heavenly Father will also forgive you. But if you do not forgive men their sins, your Father will not forgive your sins" (Matthew 6:14–15). "Be kind and compassionate to one another, forgiving each other, just as in Christ God forgave you" (Ephesians 4:32). Is it right to expect people to forgive things like sexual abuse, being abandoned by a parent, or being told continually, "You'll never amount to anything"?

If we had to forgive by using only our human resources, it would be impossible. But the God who knows everything about us and is still willing to forgive us offers the supernatural ability to forgive with our will—not our emotions. Emotions are so changeable and unstable that we can't begin to understand them, much less control them. However, it's God's miracle that sooner or later your emotions will catch up with your will to forgive. When you say, "Lord, I forgive my father—or my sister, or that teacher who always picked on me," and you mean it with all your heart, reminding yourself of your commitment to forgive whenever things get tough—someday your emotions will clear and your resentment will be gone. We're all different, so the time element will vary.

God's purpose in our forgiving one another is to free both the victim and the perpetrator of wrongdoing. The person who tells you, "I'll never forgive you for that," puts a big burden on you. If you decide not to forgive your mother, you become miserable and trapped. We just can't function very well in unforgiveness. The God-given biblical commands to forgive others are meant to help us. He didn't give us the capacity to forgive on our own because He wanted us to begin the incredible adventure of trusting God for pardoning power and everything else we need. By coming to God to receive the power to forgive, we become free and we get to know God an awfully lot better.

There are living examples everywhere that demonstrate the difference forgiveness makes. I once taught a Bible club for children. The atmosphere was contaminated by the hatred displayed by some children who were caught up in a family feud. I finally persuaded the oldest girl involved to accompany me to the home of the children she had been harassing in order to ask forgiveness. Once we arrived, the tension mounted. No one wanted to forgive and forget. It was all very awkward. Finally, a six-year-old led the way, and everybody asked for forgiveness. Later when we all walked down the street together, the children were skipping for joy. One boy unknowingly came out with a great Bible truth: "We're all so happy because we've forgiven one another." A new sense of contentment and peace pervaded the Bible club.

We've all heard people give radiant testimonies about the joy found after forgiving an abusive parent, a swindler, or even a rapist. Forgiving and being forgiven is one of the greatest things in the world. It changes our outlook on life, cures insomnia, and puts new energy into life.

It's no wonder that the devil does everything possible to keep you from asking for forgiveness. It's terribly humbling, and excuses for putting it off readily come to mind. In case you haven't caught on by now, these pretexts are sent by Satan himself. When you do decide to ask another person for forgiveness, have you ever noticed that it's never the right time, and that your mouth gets so dry the words just won't come out? Demonic resistance is tremendous. That's normal. Satan doesn't want you to enjoy that *wow-this-is-great* feeling that asking forgiveness will give you.

Don't be a wimp. Don't fall for Satan's tactics. Being willing to ask another for forgiveness is a real sign of manliness or femininity at its best. It's always a step of faith, but as you purpose to say, "I'm sorry. Will you forgive me?" God will come through with the strength. Even if the other person refuses, you'll be free. You will have done your part, and God will bless you for it.

1. *Ask for Forgiveness*

a. Ask God to bring to your mind all the people from whom you need to ask forgiveness. Even if the other person is mostly at fault, you should ask forgiveness for what *you* did. Make a list of these people.

b. Decide on the wording ahead of time—something simple like— "I'm sorry I _____

_____ .

I was wrong. Will you forgive me?" NEVER bring up the guilt of the other party. If the person doesn't want to pardon you, don't get upset. You've done your part and the Lord will take care of the rest.

c. If you've taken money, borrowed something without returning it, or damaged something, it's your biblical obligation to pay all you owe. If the amount is large, arrange manageable payments. Then you will say, "I'm sorry. I _____ and I intend to pay you back. Will you forgive me?"

d. Decide how you will ask for forgiveness.

   1. Person to person

   2. By phone—and it's well worth paying for a long-distance call

   3. By letter

e. Don't put it off. Start right away so you can begin checking names off your list. If it includes an especially tough situation, get another Christian to pray for you while you're asking for forgiveness. (Try to pick an appropriate time if you're going to talk to the person or make a phone call.)

These are all the books I checked out in Junior High... ...How much do I owe?..

Central Junior High School Library

2. Paying Back What You Have Taken or Damaged.

The Bible contains a principle called restitution. That means that if you steal or break an object or forget to return something borrowed, you are responsible to pay the owner back. The law of Moses explains this standard, applying it to animals, the most valuable property the Israelites owned.

"If a man steals an ox or a sheep and slaughters it or sells it, he must pay back five head of cattle for the ox and four sheep for the sheep" (Exodus 22:1). "If a man borrows an animal from his neighbor and it is injured or dies while the owner is not present, he must make restitution" (Exodus 22:14). The New Testament instructs us: "Let no debt remain outstanding" (Romans 13:8). You are responsible to pay for the food you ate on the sly, the book you never returned to the library, the repairing of the desk into which you chiseled your initials, and the change you swiped from your mother's purse. Even if you weren't a Christian at the time, it's still your responsibility to make it right. Sometimes there's no guilt involved because you damaged something accidentally. However, the principle of being economically responsible for the loss still applies.

    a. Ask God to help you remember what you've taken from others or in some way destroyed. Make a list of the people and the things you owe them.

    b. Start paying people back as quickly as possible so you can begin crossing names off your list.

c. If you owe an awfully lot of money, ask a mature, committed Christian to help you work out a reasonable schedule of payment. Maybe you could work for the person to pay back the debt.

YOU CAN ALWAYS AFFORD A CLEAR CONSCIENCE—NO MATTER HOW MUCH IT COSTS YOU!

When Should I Feel Guilty? **DAY 4**

Do you sometimes feel discouraged, depressed, and defeated, like you're a terrible failure as a Christian, yet you're not even sure what's wrong? Does that *I-know-I-could-do-better-but-I-can't-remember-doing-anything-really-terrible-yet-I-feel-guilty* syndrome hit you at the most unexpected times? Are there days when some vague, dark *blah* cloud seems to hang over you? Do you also experience specific pangs of conscience, like a replay of the angry words you spouted off to your mother and an insistent inner voice saying, "Talking back to your mother was sin. Confess it to God and apologize to your mom"?

When you confess your sins, which signals should you respond to? It's very important that you know the answer to this question because the devil is a liar and he spends a lot of time laying false guilt on people.

Satan's flip-flop strategy also includes trying to make teenagers totally comfortable with things that are definitely contrary to God's commandments. If he can cross the wires so you feel guilty when you're not doing anything wrong, and you accept sin as normal behavior, he can make you miserable and ruin your life. Although he'll attack you directly on this, he'll more often use the strong deception he's placed on the whole society, especially the media, to try to influence you.

There is only one way for you to straighten out your thinking. Always remember that what the Bible declares to be sin is wrong—no matter what everybody else says. But if Scripture doesn't set forth a principle that condemns the action, why should you feel guilty? It's not your fault that your parents got divorced, that your brother started taking drugs, or that Marcy decided to move in with her boyfriend. The Bible does not hold you responsible for the *decisions* of other people.

There should be no guilt attached to lack of ability, making honest mistakes, or not measuring up to the *unrealistic* standards you've set for yourself or that others have placed before you. The Bible does not say that being clumsy, singing off-key, not being able to understand math, missing the free throw that would have won the game, or losing the assignment should make you feel guilty. There's nothing wrong with being human!

If you have that vague, yucky feeling of guilt when you haven't specifically done anything that the Bible says is sin, decide that it's from the Pit and reject it decisively and firmly.

However, when the Holy Spirit convicts you of sin, it will be specific and it will have a biblical base. If you react with pride, something the Bible repeatedly condemns, confess it immediately and turn from it. The Bible declares that sex outside of marriage is wrong—no matter how many people say it's natural, or that it's the only way to express your love, or that it's necessary in order to be accepted by your peers. If you're doing it, you should feel guilty. Treat it as sin and repent. The Bible teaches, "Do nothing out of selfish ambition or vain conceit, but in humility consider others better than yourselves" (Philippians 2:3). No matter how often you're taught to assert yourself and trample on others in order to get ahead, you should feel guilty when you take advantage of people to advance yourself.

In the tricky area of when a *thought* becomes a *sin*, you must again use Scripture as your standard. Remember that it is not a sin to be tempted. The devil can put thoughts into your mind. He even gave Jesus the idea of worshiping Satan—it's no wonder he puts horrible thoughts into your brain. You need to strongly refuse these thoughts in the name of Jesus—but don't feel guilty, because they're the devil's ideas, not yours. However, they can become yours if you say, "Hey, that's right," and then continue the line of reasoning on your own. When you willfully think or act out wrong, you're sinning.

Because this area is so important, I'd like to give you three examples.

1. *The devil can give Tony thoughts and feelings of homosexuality. At that point Tony has two choices:*
   a. Tony can avoid sinning and counter with:
      1. I know a homosexual act is wrong because Leviticus 18:22 says so.
      2. Acting on my feeling would also be contrary to the scheme of God's creation and therefore unnatural, because I read that in Romans 1:26–27.

3. I don't have to panic, because I believe 1 Corinthians 10:13. "No temptation has seized you except what is common to man. And God is faithful; he will not let you be tempted beyond what you can bear. But when you are tempted, he will also provide a way out so that you can stand up under it." There is a way out, because the Bible says there is.[1]

  b. Tony has another alternative, one that will lead to disaster:

    1. He can start to agree with the devil's reasoning and choose the route Satan has planned for him. The first step is accepting the big lie swallowed by much of society: "I was born gay."

    2. Next comes the myth: "I must express my sexuality physically."

    3. And finally: "I must choose a gay lifestyle."

2. *When Darcelle sees an incredibly beautiful sweater in a store window that is totally outside her budget, the devil whispers, "You need that sweater so everyone will notice you." Here are her options:*

  a. Darcelle can let the Bible direct her response and keep clear of wrongdoing.

    1. I remember that the Word of God says, "Man looks at the outward appearance, but the Lord looks at the heart" (1 Samuel 16:7). So I'll concern myself more with what's in my heart than the clothes I wear. Friends worth keeping will like me for what I am, not for what I possess.

    2. Besides, "godliness with contentment is great gain" (1 Timothy 6:6). Lord, thanks for the clothes I do have. I won't get depressed because I can't buy the sweater. A smile will do a lot more to make me beautiful than a new sweater.

  b. Or Darcelle can choose wrong.

    1. Darcelle can accept an invitation to attend a Pit-sponsored pity-party, after which she blows up at her mother, saying, "I'm tired of being the poorest kid in school. I don't have any sharp clothes and I just have to have the pink sweater I saw in the window."

---

[1]This is a tough area, that often requires the help of competent, concerned, and committed Christians. If you or a friend need help and hope and you don't know where to turn, you can contact Exodus International, P.O. Box 2121, San Rafael, CA. 94912—phone (415) 454-1017.

2. She can even consider shoplifting.

3. *Michelle can't help hearing the worn-out Pit recording, which keeps repeating, "All you need to make you happy and fulfilled is a boyfriend." It's what she does with this thought from the enemy that counts.*

    a. She can respond with information from God's Word and turn from sinful thought patterns:

        1. Colossians 2:10 tells me, "You have been given fullness in Christ." That means that Jesus is all I need to fill up the empty spaces of loneliness and rejection in my life. Instead of an instant boyfriend, what I really need is more of Jesus.

        2. I really believe Jeremiah 29:11: " 'For I know the plans I have for you,' declares the Lord, 'plans to prosper you and not to harm you, plans to give you hope and a future.' " Lord, I'll wait until you pick out the right person for me to date. I know that any relationship outside Your will would bring me nothing but problems.

    b. Or Michelle can choose to follow the devil's thought pattern.

        1. She can say, "That's really true," and decide that since Ian is the only possibility around, she'll go out with him even if he's not a Christian.

        2. When he says he'll dump her if she doesn't have sex with him, she can convince herself that she needs a boyfriend so much that she'll give in.

In order to know when to feel guilty and when not to, you must study your Bible constantly and allow the Holy Spirit to convict you of specific sin. Scripture will also tell you what to do with your guilt. Unless you understand the purpose of God-sent guilt, you can become pretty mixed up. Like pain, genuine guilt is really a friend. Without the warning that pain gives, your infected appendix could burst and you could even die. The pain is what gives you the chance to go to the doctor, get an operation, and then resume a normal happy life.

Guilt serves you notice that you've been infected with the terrible disease called sin. The Bible will tell you whether the name of the illness is pride, greed, immorality, lying, or something else. By admitting your wrongdoing and being willing to turn from it and, if necessary, make restitution, you permit God to perform the necessary operation so you can again experience His freedom and joy.

Learn to quickly recognize a thought placed in your mind by the devil, to firmly reject it, and save yourself one of Satan's guilt trips by attributing the idea to him and not to yourself. And don't fall for the *a-dark-cloud-just-fell-on-me-I-feel-yucky-so-I-must-be-guilty-of-something* strategy. Remember that *genuine* guilt appears when you have disobeyed God. If you haven't done anything scripturally wrong, don't feel guilty.

But don't forget that the devil will also try to cover up the guilt you feel for sin you really do commit, so you won't deal with it until complications set in. Don't let the enemy get by with it. Decide to confess each sin to God *immediately*. Also make it right with the person you've sinned against.

Rejecting false guilt and dealing promptly with guilt sent by God will give you tremendous freedom. But there's no pat formula for recognizing the difference. Only staying close to God and carefully studying the Bible will give you this discernment.

1. Take a *Learning-to-Tell-the-Difference* Test.
   Should you feel guilty if:

   a. You tell your mom to say you're not home so you don't have to answer the telephone call of the kid you least want to talk to.

   Yes—No

   b. Your team lost the game because you struck out with bases loaded in the top of the ninth.

   Yes—No

   c. You know who stole the answer key to the biology test, but say nothing when the teacher asks for information.

   Yes—No

   d. Your parents fight or get a divorce.

   Yes—No

   e. You don't have any money to give in the missionary offering.

   Yes—No

f. You talk back to your mother when she's obviously wrong.

Yes—No

g. You spread some untrue rumors about a girl who has ruined your reputation with her lies.

Yes—No

2. Correct your test using the following answer key. Pay special attention to the biblical reasoning behind each answer.

Biblical answers to test:

a. "Therefore each of you must put off falsehood and speak truthfully to his neighbor, for we are all members of one body" (Ephesians 4:25). Every "little white lie" is a sin, and you should feel guilty every time you say something with the intention of deceiving. Every time you don't tell the truth, you must go through the embarrassing ordeal of confessing it to God *and* the person to whom you lied.

b. "As a father has compassion on his children, so the Lord has compassion on those who fear him; for he knows how we are formed, he remembers that we are dust" (Psalm 103:13–14). You never have to feel guilty for something you're incapable of physically, mentally, or emotionally. It's okay to be human.

c. "Acquitting the guilty and condemning the innocent—the Lord detests them both" (Proverbs 17:15). "If a person sins because he does not speak up when he hears a public charge to testify regarding something he has seen or learned about, he will be held responsible" (Leviticus 5:1). God expects that you do your part to see that justice is carried out. You should feel guilty for withholding information necessary to convict another of wrongdoing. Telling on a classmate for cheating, stealing, or beating up on somebody is one of the hardest things God will ask of you as a teenager in today's world.

d. "The soul who sins is the one who will die. The son will not share the guilt of the father, nor will the father share the guilt of the son" (Ezekiel 18:20). Obviously, if the whole argument started because you took the car without permission and wrecked it, you should feel guilty for *your* actions. Ask for forgiveness, and pay for at least part of the damage. But aside from that, this verse sets forth a very important biblical principle: You are never responsible for the decisions of others. You can't blame your parents for your sin, and they can't blame you for theirs. Don't you feel guilty for what someone else does.

e. "For if the willingness is there, the gift is acceptable according to what one has, not according to what he does not have" (2 Corinthians 8:12). If the reason you have no money for the announced Sunday missionary offering is that you blew your whole paycheck on Friday, you should feel guilty. But if you're really broke and can't put anything in the collection plate or buy an expensive Christmas gift for your mom or pitch in to buy something for your Sunday-school teacher, don't feel guilty. God judges your heart's generosity, not the size of your pocketbook.

f. "Honor your father and your mother" (Exodus 20:12). "Do not let any unwholesome talk come out of your mouths, but only what is helpful for building others up according to their needs, that it may benefit those who listen" (Ephesians 4:29). You should feel guilty, because even if you're right it's your responsibility to express yourself in such a way as to honor your mother and build her up.

g. "You shall not give false testimony against your neighbor" (Exodus 20:16). "But I tell you that men will have to give account on the day of judgment for every careless word they have spoken" (Matthew 12:36). You should feel guilty not only for lying but for trying to play God. The Bible teaches: "Do not take revenge, my friend, but leave room for God's wrath, for it is written: 'It is mine to avenge; I will repay,' says the Lord" (Romans 12:19).

These examples should give you some idea of how to apply Scripture to the area of guilt. Don't hesitate to ask a mature Christian, who knows the Bible better than you do, to help you find the verses that apply to your situation.

Forgiveness Is for Keeps

DAY 5

If you're making a long-distance phone call to Tibet, or trying to whisper across the classroom, or shouting instructions to a friend who won't turn down his radio—then you know the frustration. You say the same thing over and over to make sure the message gets through. And you've been on the other end of overkill conversations as well. Your math teacher repeats the assignment seven times in hopes that someone will remember to do it. Does your mom ever sound like a broken record when she explains what she wants done? Don't worry. That means she's a normal mother and that you're a typical teenager, not especially noted for your ability to follow directions!

But you're getting the point: Constant repetition implies lack of confidence in the listener's ability to hear or willingness to act. If you're still praying—"Lord, forgive me for the candy bar I stole from the corner store five years ago, for knocking down my little sister's snowman when I was in sixth grade, and for cheating on the test on fractions"—then you don't understand God's forgiveness. When we agree with God that we've sinned, and we do what is humanly possible to make things right with the person we've wronged and then turn from our sins, God not only forgives—*He* forgets. "I, even I, am he who blots out your transgressions, for my own sake, and remembers your sins no more" (Isaiah 43:25). "The blood of Jesus, his Son, purifies us from all sin" (1 John 1:7). And it disappears!

But you might say, "I believe He'll totally forgive all that kid stuff, but you don't know what I've done—I've had an abortion." "I was part of a group that did hundreds of dollars worth of vandalism." "I fathered a child, and I don't even know where he is." "I've shoplifted enough stuff to start a store." "I've literally given my mother an ulcer." But God is great, and *He* can forgive anything. He can and He *will.* That includes sins like murder, which you can't in any way undo. God totally and completely forgives the person who repents of wrongdoing—no matter how terrible the offense. Although some scars may remain, God will erase the pain and the guilt.

The miracle of Christianity is not only that the sins of those who put their trust in Christ are wiped clean, enabling them to spend eternity in heaven, but the person also gets a new start so that he or she can enjoy complete freedom here on earth.

You don't have to ask God for forgiveness over and over again for the same sin. When your heart is sincere, God forgives you the first time, and His forgiveness has no strings attached. It is His will that you resist all the accusations Satan will throw at you concerning past sins that you've already confessed. When you still feel guilty after making things right with God and others—throw the whole thing back in Satan's face. His agenda is to make you feel *yucky*, and to steal your joy by rehashing finished business with God. Be smart enough not to put up with it.

Remember: You're not just free on bail—*you're free*! You never again need to return to the prison that sin had placed around you. Because they acted like forgiven people, God used Paul, the former persecutor of Christians; John Newton, once a slave trader; and Nicky Cruz, an ex-gang member. The church is made up of people who used to lie, take drugs, sleep around, and step on others to get to the top. But God's forgiveness changes people. There's a song that affirms that if all you have is God, you have enough to start over again. That's true. Take the gift of His forgiveness, never look back, and serve the Lord with all your heart—refusing to let the memories of forgiven sin stand in your way.

Steps TO TAKE

Sometimes a specific ceremony helps us visualize a commitment and record it forever. Although you could do this alone, I'd suggest you invite a good friend to share the experience with you.

1. Spend about fifteen minutes in complete silence before God. Have a pencil, and a paper with two columns, along with your Bible. As you pray, asking God to refresh your memory, write down in column

one the forgiven sins for which you still sometimes feel guilty. In column two, record any unconfessed sin that God brings to mind—immediately confessing it.

2. Then thank God for His forgiveness—and burn the papers, symbolizing that you and the Lord are forgetting about these sins.

Chapter Ten
But That's Not What I Want to Hear

If you're really going to follow Jesus, you're going to have to become a disciplined person!...

When Trent came home from Bible camp, he was ready to turn the world upside down for Jesus. He'd rededicated his life to the Lord and felt God was calling him to be a pastor. Working hard in his church, he channeled his enthusiasm and boundless energy into whatever seemed most exciting at the moment.

He convinced almost every kid in the youth group to join the pro-life march and organized a picnic afterward. Then he put his heart into planning extravagant evangelistic socials for the youth group. But when the second one fizzled, he decided to join the door-to-door evangelism team. At first, he really depended on God and saw several people accept Christ. But the routine of it all and the North Dakota winter weather caused him to look for greener pastures. All the while, he was neglecting his schoolwork, sluffing off on jobs his parents assigned to him, and ignoring his little sisters.

One night his parents had a serious talk with him.

"Trent," his father began, "we're very happy to see you involved in church and choosing the right kind of friends. But you keep jumping from one thing to another, and your grades are suffering."

"We're so proud that you're thinking about the ministry," his mother said, "and we know that Christian work demands discipline and the ability to stick with whatever you start. You aren't developing these qualities. We'd like to help you."

Trent was stunned. He was always thought of as a "super-Christian." After all, he was doing the Lord's work, and to him homework didn't seem to be very "spiritual."

His father saw the look on his face and interrupted his thoughts. "A young man of your ability shouldn't be sliding by with a C average. The sidewalk hasn't been shoveled for three weeks, and you didn't even do this week's lesson for the Bible study course you're taking."

"But, Dad," Trent countered, "you know I'm the star of the Christmas play, and we've been practicing every other night. Really, I don't think worldly knowledge is all that important. Besides, I read my Bible lesson, even if I didn't fill it out."

"Son, until you learn diligence and responsibility, God will never be able to use you effectively," his father affirmed quietly. "I'm ordering you to shovel off the walk now—and asking you to think about what we said."

Trent obediently started the snow-removal project, all the while feeling that his parents didn't correctly understand God's priorities. "Most adults," he reasoned, "are very materialistic, so they emphasize things like good grades and always getting your work done on time. If the Lord comes back next week, it won't make the slightest difference whether I can explain photosynthesis, or know who wrote *Moby Dick*."

For Sunday, their church had invited a famous guest speaker and his topic was: "Listening to God." He began by saying, "Many people do not fully believe that God speaks today. If we think we get direction only through Scripture, then we will miss out on much of what God has to share, because He will speak so often through His Spirit, circumstances, and other people. We must make absolutely certain that we are fully convinced and persuaded that God does speak to us personally about our families, our businesses, our finances, our hurts, our frustrations, and our fears."[1] The visiting pastor recommended three things:

1. After your daily Bible reading, sit in quietness before the Lord for five minutes to let the Holy Spirit impress something on your heart.

2. Take notes in Sunday school class, Bible studies, and church services, because God may want to say something directly to you through these teachers of His Word.

3. When you're facing difficult or unusual circumstances, ask God what He wants to teach you through the experience.

Trent was all pumped up to listen to God. He decided he'd ask God to show him specifically whether or not he was called to be a pastor. When he talked it over with Steve, his youth group leader, Trent excitedly exclaimed, "And maybe God will even send an angel to tell me!"

Steve smiled knowingly and asked: "Trent, approximately how many years passed between the events recorded in Chapter 12 of Genesis, when God called Abraham, and the writing of Revelation, Chapter 22?" Trent had no idea. Steve said, "The answer is—a little over 2000 years. How many people do you think God was dealing with during that time? How many of them saw angels? Not very many, right? God is God and He can do whatever He wants, but His

[1]Charles Stanley, *Listening to God*, Nelson Audio Library, side 4.

most common ways of talking to us are through the Bible, through the still small voice of His Spirit, through circumstances, and through other people. Once you start *looking for visions of angels*, instead of sincerely seeking to hear God's voice however He wishes to speak to you, the door is opened for satanic deception. Hearing from God should be your goal. You don't need some exotic experience to go along with it."

That calmed Trent down a little, and he brought a notebook and pen to the Wednesday night service with the intention of taking notes. But what the pastor was saying made him uncomfortable: "Unless you are a diligent worker, God will never be able to use you. Even if you're sincere, talented, and well-versed in Scripture, you'll burn out without perseverance and hard work."

Trent stopped writing in the middle of the sentence and started drawing the robots he was famous for in sixth grade. His sermon note-taking had bombed, but he thought the *chapter-a-day-plus-listening* remedy might rescue his self-image. He read the first chapter of 1 Corinthians and attempted to sit quietly for five minutes. But after one minute and 48 seconds, which seemed like an eternity, he flipped on his CD player, vowing that tomorrow's period of silence would last a little longer and that he'd gradually work up to five minutes.

On the fourth day, he read something that really grabbed his attention. During his short time of concentrating on listening to God, the words of that verse kept coming back to him: "Now it is required that those who have been given a trust must prove faithful" (1 Corinthians 4:2). The only "visions" he had were of an unshoveled sidewalk, a half-written English theme, and an unkept promise to his little sister, Jessica. Instead of doing the work his parents had assigned to him, completing the composition, and making plans to take Jessica to the zoo on Saturday, he flicked on the TV with the excuse that God didn't seem very interested in telling him whether or not he should be a pastor.

Trent then turned his full attention to a project designed to put a Christian comic book into the hands of every student at Armstrong High. The idea was to pass them out to students as they left the school grounds at 3:00 P.M. Trent and Debbie were given the street next to the teachers' parking lot. When the juniors' counselor, Mr. Perkins, walked by, Trent smiled. "I could give you a free comic book too," he joked. "Would it be beneath your dignity to read it?"

"Not at all," the amiable Mr. Perkins had replied. "I might even like it."

Trent thought no more about it until his homeroom teacher handed him a slip, asking him to make an appointment with Mr. Perkins. Wondering what was up, he arranged to see him that afternoon.

Mr. Perkins closed the door to his office, cleared his throat, and began. "Trent, I just don't have any respect for religious fanatics like yourself. You can pass out propaganda like mad, pull off a sensational religious speech in English class—and at the same time earn shamefully low grades. It's actually remarkable that a kid as smart as you are can come up with such a terrible report card. Mrs. Doyle asked me to talk to you. She feels she's wasting her time on you. She wants you transferred to honors English where you'll flunk if you don't do the work. I called your parents, and they agree with Mrs. Doyle. What have you got to say about it?"

Trent, for once in his life, was speechless. He sputtered something about needing a couple of days to think it over and asked if he could leave. Once out in the hall, he realized that God had tried in many ways to get his attention. But because he hadn't wanted to face the consequences, he'd blocked out God's voice. If he'd only realized it and had been willing to listen, he would have received God's instructions the first time He spoke—through his parents.

God had quite a lot for Trent to learn before he could even think of becoming a pastor.

YOU HAVE AN APPOINTMENT WITH THE CREATOR OF THE UNIVERSE...

...to learn strategies for listening to God.

All Ears!

DAY 1

Very few things get the attention of everyone—a fire alarm, an air raid siren, a lady in a bathing suit riding an elephant down main street, perhaps—but certainly not spoken words or written instructions. Communication breaks down all the time. Often it is because we didn't pay careful attention to the things we were being told.

Real listening requires a lot of active energy. It's something few people know how to do—just look around your classroom during a teacher's lecture and you'll see what I mean! Most kids easily tune out a parent's scolding, instructor's assignment, a *when-I-was-a-boy* comparison, plus anything else they don't happen to be particularly interested in. Some couldn't concentrate on totally listening for ten minutes even if their lives depended on it.

The reason so many teenagers—and adults—hear nothing from God is that they tune Him out just like everyone else. Listening isn't that easy, but you can learn the necessary skills.

The first thing to get straight is that *you* don't call the shots. God does. You can't dictate to Him when or how to speak to you. You can't just request that God send you a dream in technicolor every time He has something to tell you, that He install a heavenly MTV channel for you to tune in at your leisure, or send an angel each time He has a message for you. He is God and He will decide when and how to communicate with you.

As He did so often in the New Testament, God will speak to you through His Spirit. An impression from the Holy Spirit indicated to Peter that Ananias and Sapphira were lying about the amount of money they sold the property for; prompted Philip to approach the Ethiopian in his chariot to witness to him; led Peter to go with the men Cornelius had sent; caused the church at Antioch to choose Paul and Barnabas as missionaries; and kept Paul from preaching in Asia.

We know that Peter had just been up on the roof praying before he received instructions from the Holy Spirit, and while the Antioch church was fasting and praying, they sensed God wanted them to send out two missionaries. My guess is that Philip was meditating on God's Word—not thinking about the Roman circus as he walked along the road that day, and that Paul had opened his heart to the Holy Spirit's voice by spending time with God.

You can't be receptive to God's still small voice if your mind is buzzing with finishing the English assignment, impressing that certain someone, hurrying to get to school on time, trying out for the team, and planning a ski weekend. You need to take *time* to quiet down—five minutes to a half an hour. At first this may seem impossible and pointless. While God may be working on the inside of you, it will probably take a while before you learn to enjoy spending time with Him and sense His Holy Spirit giving you the specific guidance you need. When you stop rushing around and sit still, you make it possible for God to get your attention.

Have you ever wished that someone cared enough about you to want to spend unhurried time alone with you? Wouldn't you like to be so important to someone that time with you was top priority—no excuses to get going, no urgent business to attend to, no impatience with hearing your story over and over again? There is Someone like that. God loves you so much He wants you all to himself. It's up to you to find a place and a time to meet with Him without competition and distracting noise. Often the only possibility of this kind of stillness is early in the morning or late at night. Morning is usually best because your mind isn't filled with the problems of the day and no one will disturb your tranquility at 6:00 A.M. If you want Him to show you His love, shower you with His peace, share His secrets and guide your life, you have to make the appointments.

One of the biggest obstacles to hearing from God in our modern age is that our minds are so cluttered with garbage that we can't really distinguish His voice. If you've been watching horror videos, soaking in hours of TV, endlessly playing Super-Nintendo and listening a lot to secular music, your mind will be so full of junk that God won't be able to get a word in edgewise. Tune-in to your local Christian radio station, buy some CDs by artists who know Jesus as Savior—and above all, spend some time reading the Bible and good Christian books. Clear out the trash, so that impressions sent by God are not drowned out.

God wants to speak to us directly through the Bible. Be an active listener by taking notes on each sermon and Bible-talk you hear, participating in the discussions in your Sunday school class or Bible study. Devote some special time into digging into God's Word and read a Scripture passage each day. Very often God will apply its words to your specific situation. Open your Bible expecting God to speak to you. It's a good idea to have a notebook and pen ready to write down some specific insights you get from God's Word. Even if you don't find a verse which tells you whether or not to accept the part-time job offer, filling your mind with Scripture will enable you to better discern what God wants to tell you through His Spirit, other people, or circumstances.

Like Trent, you may not realize how much God wants to teach you through your parents, your teachers, and others in authority over you. When someone criticizes you, instead of immediately defending yourself, ask God if there's some truth in what was said. Ask Him if you should change in some way. In some cases it would be wise for you to ask a trusted Christian friend to evaluate the unfavorable comments about your character honestly. Don't become so proud that you shut out the things God wants to tell you through other people.

It's true that some circumstances are arranged by the devil. Job's catastrophe, the temptation of Jesus, and Paul's "thorn in the flesh" are biblical examples. But you must also remember that God *permitted* Satan to cause these painful situations. When trials come we pray that God will bail us out. That is the right thing to do. But we should also ask a question: "Lord, what do you want me to learn through this ordeal?" If you charge your way into a financial jam, God's first step toward giving you prosperity will be teaching you how to manage money. If you didn't crack a book all month, it is very doubtful that God will supernaturally give you the answers to the test questions. Often

God tries to get our attention through unusual or difficult circumstances, but we're just not listening.

If you really start taking notes in church, set aside priority time to sit quietly before God, carefully evaluate what others say to you, and try to learn God's lessons from each circumstance, some people might think you're a little weird. But if you don't, you'll miss out on a lifetime of heavy-duty blessings like:

1. Seeing God clear up your confusion.
2. Finding the security niche God has for you while the storms of life rage.
3. Exchanging sadness and pessimism for joy and peace.
4. Discovering friendship with God as the cure for your loneliness.
5. Confessing your sinfulness and rebellion in order to experience forgiveness and the release of flowing with God's purposes.
6. Replacing insecurity with God's rock-solid reality.
7. Getting clear direction in chaotic situations.

No matter how messed up the world gets, no one can ever take from you "the secret place with God" that you build by forming habits that enable you to listen to what He wishes to tell you.

1. Use this chart to evaluate your listening habits this week.

2. It would be a good idea to make copies of this chart so you could check your progress week after week. (Few people would say that Christians should never watch TV, etc., but one must use discretion and limit the time spent in front of the boob-tube.)

Listening Habits—How Did You Do This Week?

Did You Take Notes?	Junk Food Diet	Spiritual Vitamins	Advice, Correction	Difficult or unusual circumstances (including unusual blessings):
☐ Sunday morning service ☐ Youth meeting ☐ Bible study ☐ Other services	Hours of TV ____ Hours of secular music ____ Hours of secular videos and movies ____	Hours of Christian music ____ Hours of Christian TV or radio ____ Time invested in: Bible reading ____ listening to God ____ prayer ____ reading Christian books ____	Criticism Received: ____ ____ ____ ____ ____ Did you: ☐ Pray about it? ☐ Confirm it with appropriate scripture? ☐ Get mature Christian advice?	1. ____ 2. ____ 3. ____ 4. ____ Did you ask God what you are to learn from these things?

You Are What You Think   DAY 2

An old saying goes like this: "That which exists in the well of your thoughts will sooner or later come up in the bucket of your speech." What we mull over in our minds also spills over into our actions. It's no wonder that the mind is the world's greatest battlefield. If the devil can infiltrate your thoughts, he's on his way to winning—and you're on your way to sinning!

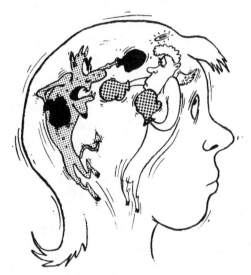

There are some techniques that can be used either for good or for evil. Hopefully you've been warned about Eastern meditation and chanting, which forces one to concentrate on pagan deities and false teaching, with the goal of achieving a state in which all thinking ceases—opening the mind up to demonic forces! Any physical benefit of this kind of meditation is completely offset by very real dangers.

However, there is also what I call *chewing-the-cud-Bible-meditation* using repetition of scriptural truth, which can help you to relax and focus your mind on God. Like the contented cow, that probably enjoys its food more and for a longer time than any animal, your concentrating and refocusing on a little piece of Scripture can give you immense satisfaction and peace of mind. The goal of Christian meditation is *never* a blank mind. It is *not* some good work engaged in to gain God's favor. It is rather hiding God's Word in our hearts so we won't sin against Him. It is consciously putting our minds on God's truth so we don't soak in the humanistic thinking all around us. It is digesting Scripture chunk-by-chunk and making it part of us.

When you feel like taking revenge, refuse to take your eyes off the words "Love your enemies, do good to those who hate you" (Luke 6:27) until that message melts the feelings of anger and resentment and you come up with a specific plan to put it into practice. If you're really upset and about to do something rash, say out loud, "Be still and know that I am God," (Psalm 46:10) over and over until you sense that the Lord of the universe is perfectly capable of handling your problem. As you face seemingly irresistible temptation, making a little song out of "When you are tempted, he will also provide a way out" can save you from buying Satan's *I've-got-you-this-time* lie.

Other times, meditating on Scripture is like putting money in the bank for future use. The verses you over-memorize will stay with you forever. If you go to sleep repeating "Give thanks in all circumstances" (1 Thessalonians 5:18), your dreams and the waking moments of your tomorrow may be quite different than if you used your *drifting-off-to-dreamland* time planning a tantrum to force your dad to let you have the car Friday night! Having firmly entrenched that biblical principle in your memory and your value system, it will come back to you when you need it most.

Total concentration on a phrase from Scripture is a good way to relax. It's different from reading or studying, which is more like work. You've probably noticed that some of the devil's worst attacks come when your mind isn't fully in gear. Forming a habit of chewing on a short little phrase of God's Word can give your mind the rest it needs and keep out demonic interference at the same time.

Isaiah 26:3 is a key concept: "Thou wilt keep him in perfect peace, whose mind is stayed on thee: because he trusteth in thee" (KJV). Or in today's English: "You will keep in perfect peace him whose mind is steadfast, because he trusts in you." It's the *not-so-secret* formula for peace of mind. Obviously, you can't read the Bible all day long, nor can you sit around all day thinking about God. But if you take five minutes each day to concentrate on a phrase or sentence of Scripture, you can pull it out and chew on it during every moment your mind isn't occupied doing a math problem, studying for the history test, or giving change to a customer. You can walk to your locker repeating, "Godliness with contentment is great gain" (1 Timothy 6:6). You can iron your clothes singing to yourself, "God opposes the proud but gives grace to the humble" (James 4:6). You can wait at the bus stop, letting "So do not fear: for I am with you" (Isaiah 41:10) run through your mind like one of those neon signs that constantly repeats its message.

This isn't some gimmick, however. If your relationship with Jesus isn't vital enough so you can truly trust Him, your "meditation" could be just playing word games. The Bible only comes to life if we have a love relationship with the Author. If you've ever fallen in love, you know how you hang on every word spoken by that special someone. You think the jokes are funny, the stories interesting, and the ideas fantastic. Love and trust go together. You trust the person because you love him or her, and you love because you trust.

Only if you love and trust Jesus completely can His promises produce faith and dissolve fear. To some people "For God so loved the world" means nothing, but to those of us who have experienced that wonderful love personally, it's a beautiful reminder of what our Savior has done for us and what He wants to do for every person on earth. Fall in love with Jesus and let His words bring you the peace, joy, comfort, and truth that you need.

Steps TO TAKE

Suggestions for meditating on 1 Peter 5:7: "Cast all your anxiety on him because he cares for you."

1. Read the verse out loud several times.

2. Read it out loud, emphasizing a different word each time: CAST all your anxiety on him because he cares for you. Cast ALL your anxiety on him because he cares for you, etc.

3. Write it out a couple of times.

4. Picture the recommended action in your mind as you repeat the verse, exchanging the word anxiety with what's bothering you at the moment:

Cast all your worries about passing algebra on Him because He cares about you.

Cast all your concern about being popular on Him because He cares about you, etc.

5. Describe the actions of the God who cares about you by adding phrases to the end of the verse as a way to make it personal:

I will cast all my cares on Him because He cares for me *by giving me a friend like Carla.*

I will cast all my cares on Him because He cares for me *by providing a good Bible study to attend.*

I will cast all my cares on Him because He cares for me *by loving me even when no one else does.*

6. Using a tune you know or one you make up, sing the verse a few times or invent a rap rhythm for repeating the verse.

7. Read the verse silently a few times, just enjoying its rich meaning.

8. Remember the verse whenever your mind isn't fully occupied, and repeat it to yourself throughout the day.

9. Choose other short verses or parts of verses and go through each of these steps. Try these for starters:

a. "A gentle answer turns away wrath" (Proverbs 15:1).

b. "Trust in the Lord and do good" (Psalm 37:3).

c. "When I am afraid, I will trust in you" (Psalm 56:3).

d. "The word of the Lord stands firm forever" (1 Peter 1:25).

e. "Pour out your hearts to him, for God is our refuge" (Psalm 62:8).

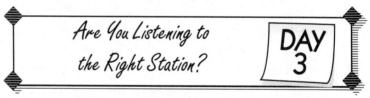

Are You Listening to the Right Station?

DAY 3

Thousands of thoughts flit through your mind each day: "I want almond-fudge instead of strawberry." "He sure is a bore." "Lord, that flower you made is sensational." "Maybe the only way to get a good grade is to cheat." "I know Jesus would want me to love her anyway." Your ideas can be influenced by Satan, come from God, or originate in your own mind. How do you tell the difference?

Some people flippantly declare things like, "The Lord told me to find another youth group," or, "I heard from God, and I'm dropping chemistry." It's very possible to substitute what we want to do for instructions that really do come from God. On the other extreme, there are those who are so fearful of making a mistake that they're never certain God has spoken to them. They expect nothing and they get it every time. To add to the confusion, Satan masquerades as an angel of light trying to make us think his ideas are really from God. How can we recognize when God talks to us?

First of all, we need a right relationship with God and a willingness to obey Him. If you're unwilling to forgive your father, the devil can easily talk you into not respecting him. When you're hiding out from God because of a sin you won't admit, Satan's solutions seem very logical. Pride blurs God's reality. Besides, God won't waste His breath if you've already decided not to obey Him. Unless you're walking close to Him, ready to do what He tells you, forget about hearing from Him.

The acid test of any idea you feel you've received from God is this: *Is it consistent with Scripture?* When the Bible says "Do not be yoked together with unbelievers" (2 Corinthians 6:14), you know God will *never* "lead" you to marry a non-Christian. Scripture declares, "Children, obey your parents in the Lord" (Ephesians 6:1), and "Do everything without complaining or arguing" (Philippians 2:14). So your decision to make a stand against having to do three hours of housework every Saturday can't be from God. "Do to others what you would have them do to you" (Matthew 7:12) means that the Lord did *not* tell you never to speak to Shauna again.

There are many times when we should check what we feel God is telling us to do with some mature committed Christian. Pray about it, too, and don't rush into anything. Some of the best advice I've ever received is this: "God's will today will still be God's will tomorrow. Take some time and check it out." There is a tremendous difference between unwillingness to obey God and caution that just wants to make *sure* before acting. God has a great deal of patience and will confirm His will for those who really want to do it. A sudden impulse to act *now* is usually from the devil. He has tricked many well-meaning Christians with the *if-you're-going-to-obey-God-you've-got-to-act-now* routine. It's his purpose to provoke rash action because he knows you'd never fall for his trap if you thought things through. There are emergencies in which obeying God requires immediate measures but they are rare.

Although there may be a struggle in coming to the decision, doing God's will is accompanied by a deep inner peace. Most of the devil's thoughts and propositions give feelings of agitation, compulsion, and frenzy. That *I-can't-stand-it-anymore-I've-got-to-do-something-I'm-not-sure-what-but-I'll-try-anything* feeling should flash a blinking red warning sign. It means that you must stop and spend both *quantity* and *quality* time with God in order to straighten out the confusion.

It has been said, "Taking the easy way is what makes rivers and men crooked." Usually, satanic suggestions help us get our own way at the expense of others. His advice encourages us to bypass integrity and hard work to earn easy money, gives us excuses to play the game of life by our own set of rules, or provides us a scheme for being noticed and applauded. The Bible, however, is full of things like complete surrender to God, loving your brother *and* your enemy, encouraging one another, not causing someone else to stumble, giving to the poor, and bearing one another's burdens. None of these fits very well with doing what comes naturally. So much of following God requires sacrifice, courage, and diligence. You should seriously question a call to a beach ministry in Hawaii or a desire to be rich and famous for Jesus. What God tells you to do will always fit in with *all* the principles laid down in Scripture, and will seldom be exactly what you planned anyway.

The enemy will appeal to our pride—thoughts like: "You should really be youth group president instead of Brett." "People never pay much attention to you." "Everybody's got it in for you, or they would have followed your suggestion." "If no one is going to show any more appreciation for what you do than that, just quit," These are variations on themes the devil has used successfully for centuries. Another of his lines is to lead you to believe that you, or a group you are part of, has a new insight from God or secret knowledge that no one else possesses. The scenario goes something like this: "Just think, the Bible has been around in complete form for almost 2000 years, and you're the first person/group to discover this hidden truth that will revolutionize the world." You are extremely important to God and to all humanity as a member of the body of Christ, and you don't need to fall for such nonsense in order to feel significant.

That doesn't mean that God won't show you new things from Scripture that *you've* never seen before. He will. He may use you to impart this to others who haven't noticed them yet either. But keep in mind that Bible students the world over and throughout the ages have had the same Holy Spirit to teach them truth from the Word of God.

Probably everybody likes a big emotional rush—that roller-coaster tingle in the stomach, that *I'm-hopelessly-in-love* feeling, or the thrill of a lifetime opportunity. And it is true that God does give us some emotionally stimulating times. It's great to be singing praises with everyone else and to feel God's presence. God is God. He can, and He does, give His children supernatural experiences—sometimes accompanied by lots of excitement.

It's very dangerous, however, to confuse emotions with reality. For one person, conversion to Christ is a supercharged dramatic event, and for another it might be very quiet and matter-of-fact. Although what is outwardly evident in the two cases is very different, the inward reality is the same. There are dangers in *looking for* emotional experience instead of seeking God, however He may choose to reveal himself. If we're counting on some big rush, the devil is capable of supplying it. If you're hearing literal voices, they can be satanic.

The same caution must be exercised with dreams and visions. A study of people who have taught false doctrines throughout the centuries will show you how the devil has sometimes used dreams and visions to convince people to accept ideas that completely contradict Scripture. Just because it seems miraculous is no guarantee that it comes from God. Be sure you follow God and His revelation in the Bible—not *your* emotions, or *your* dreams and visions.

You must be aware of the pitfalls in order to avoid them, but don't give up on hearing from God. Letting God speak to you is an exciting adventure. If you've prayed, aligned your life with God's will, have pure motives, find the direction consistent with Scripture and the wisdom of other mature Christians, then knowing that God wants you to do something is one of the greatest feelings in the world.

One such experience is significant to me personally. Teaching positions were scarce and I'd prayed a lot about what to do. Suddenly I got two job offers in one day! When I stepped into the dingy halls of Edison High School, I was certain that God wanted me to turn down a higher paying job in the suburbs to teach there. Only afterward did I discover that I'd escaped a terrible interview that other new teachers described as an ordeal, because the guy who was to interview me had been on vacation. Later I learned the reason I'd been chosen, even though there was a fat file of applications—a group of Christian students were praying for an advisor for the Christian club they wanted to start. I knew *God* had placed me in that school and I felt special—awed by how He had arranged "impossible" circumstances to put me where He wanted me to be.

Learn to listen to God. You'll be glad you did.

Steps TO TAKE

1. Write down one or two things you feel God is impressing on your heart. _____

_____

_____.

2. Ask yourself the question: Did God say _____?
and answer it by using the following tests to find out.

    a. Is your lifeline tuned in to God's frequency so that you're presently in a position to hear from God?

        1. Have you gotten rid of all the *Lord-don't-ask-me-to-do-that-because-I-won't* issues?

        2. Are you free from a *this-is-what-I-want-God-to-tell-me-and-it's-the-only-thing-I'll-listen-to* attitude?

        3. Are you willing to let God instruct you however He pleases?

        4. Are you reading the Bible regularly?

        5. Are you praying and spending quiet time with the Lord?

        6. Have you confessed and forsaken every known sin?

    b. Does the message pass the acid test?

        1. Does it square with the biblical doctrine that God (Father, Son, and Holy Spirit—three persons, one unity) is totally superior to you, a mere human and part of His creation who will never become some kind of a god?

        2. Is it consistent with the biblical teachings to "serve one another in love" (Galatians 5:13), "Love your neighbor as yourself" (Galatians 5:14), "Love your enemies" (Matthew 5:44), and "Honor one another above yourselves" (Romans 12:10)?

    c. Does it uphold every one of the Ten Commandments, plus every other doctrine and command in the Bible?

    d. Do other mature, consistent Christians agree that this idea could have come from God? (Obviously, this doesn't apply to the little daily decisions of life.)

God Is Speaking— Are You Listening?

DAY 4

God didn't stop talking to His people the minute the Bible was finished. He isn't sitting smugly up in heaven while some poor soul is trying to find a verse that will indicate whether or not to buy the blue jeans on the half-price sale, or whether or not joining the swim team is a good idea. It isn't true that He's only interested in the big areas of life, where He has given specific scriptural instructions. Jesus assures us, "Even the very hairs on your head are all numbered" (Matthew 10:30).

You are important to God, and He wants to guide you in every area of your life—if you're prepared to listen to whatever means He uses—His Holy Spirit, another person, circumstances, or the Bible. As the Holy Spirit makes Scripture applicable to you personally, He could use a verse such as "Bring the whole tithe into the storehouse" (Malachi 3:10) to remind that you haven't given Him any money for three weeks and that using all your money to buy a pair of Levi's you don't need is putting Him in second place.

The devil may try to convince you that you're not very important, that what you do doesn't really matter, and that God would never take the time to specifically show you His will. Don't believe it! Each one who gives his or her life totally to God can make a significant difference. Decide to be a person who changes your world—and you can only do that if you listen to God.

Another *from-the-Pit* big lie is that God is a big meany, a super killjoy who'll only yell and scream at you like authority figures who've hurt you. Because the devil runs such a successful propaganda campaign, a lot of people are scared of God. They wouldn't want to hear from Him. They're afraid. But the truth is, God has *your* best interests in mind. Communicating with Him is a wonderful investment of time and energy.

Obviously, if you're leading a double life, you're aware that seriously getting in touch with God would blow your cover. If you're rebellious or proud, you probably wouldn't even answer a long-distance phone call from heaven! If you have a *nobody's-gonna-tell-me-what-to-do* hang-up, you might as well steer clear of the Almighty. However, you could also

come to the conclusion that since God went to all the trouble to create you and send Jesus to die for you, He really does love you a lot! And it would only be sensible to want to hear instructions from the One who knows everything there is to know and really cares about you.

In order to do that, you need to develop some good listening habits. Jesus told an interesting parable about how people hear God's Word. When the sower threw out his seed, which represents the Word of God, the results depended on the condition of the soil into which it fell. What God has to tell you will never sink in if you have a listening problem.

The story Jesus told describes some hindrances to hearing from God.

Some seed fell on a path that was so packed down that the seed couldn't penetrate. This represents a closed mind. This person has already decided what he or she wants to listen to and what to tune out. Sometimes it takes a lot to get our attention. I remember a teenager who gave up on Christianity and became very cynical and bitter. In quick succession he had three serious automobile accidents in which he was not hurt, but his attitude remained unchanged. I shuddered, wondering what God would have to do to get through to him. Closing your mind to what God is trying to tell you is very dangerous.

The seed that fell on rocky places did sprout—but the thin layer of soil on top of the rocks didn't allow the roots to grow deeper, so the little plants eventually died. The people described here are cloudy-minded hearers. They'll gladly accept God's Word—or anything else—but it's all very superficial. Unless a relationship with God is deepened by serious Bible study to find out who God is and what He wants of us, it's easy to stray off into the showy, the thrilling, or the exotic. If you don't sink your roots deeply into biblical principles and realize that Jesus isn't a temporary rush—He's the "way, the truth and the life"—you may mistake another voice for His own. If a plant or a tree doesn't have deep roots, any little storm can topple it. If you're not anchored in biblical truth, the winds of adversity could destroy your flimsy faith.

The thorny-soil people are those who have cluttered minds. Their thoughts are so full of impressing members of the opposite sex, school activities, homework, money, and possessions that listening to God isn't possible. There's just too much competition, too much busyness, too much noise to even pay attention to a Sunday sermon, much less take the time to be alone with God. When your dad can't put down the evening paper long enough to listen to you, or when your friend doesn't want to talk to you on the phone because he'll miss part of his favorite TV show, you feel hurt. How does God feel when He tries to talk to you?

But take heart. You can learn to be an alert listener.[2]

Steps TO TAKE

1. You can come to church well rested with an *I-know-God-has-something-to-say-to-me-today-and-I-don't-want-to-miss-it* attitude. You can buy a notebook and take notes so you'll remember what was said.

2. Prepare your Sunday school lesson ahead of time and participate in class. You can ask questions and get your youth pastor to teach you how to do some Bible research. Take part in the discussions in your Bible study or Sunday school class. If you don't understand the meaning of a certain verse, do some investigation or ask a serious Bible student. If you think the Holy Spirit has impressed something on your mind, check it out with Scripture.

3. Be alert to events and/or statements that can confirm to you that God has spoken, and you're on the right track.

---

[2] Many ideas for this section have been adapted from Charles Stanley's book on tape, *How to Listen to God*, Nelson Audio Library.

4. Respond to what you hear by putting it into practice. Buy flowers for your mom; apologize to your friend; clean your room without being told, or whatever God is asking you to do. Obey instantly.

God does want to guide you through this difficult and dangerous life. He wants to warn you of pitfalls, direct you through the fog, and tell you He loves you. If you don't take the time and trouble to learn to be a good listener, you'll miss out on so much.

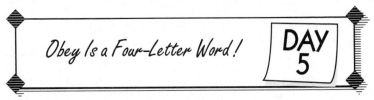

Obey Is a Four-Letter Word! DAY 5

Every teenage generation from the dawn of time has heard it: "The young people of today are going to the dogs." Although that means different things to different people, it's always negative. And you'd have to admit that sexual promiscuity, drug use, disrespect for authority, crime, and shoplifting are on the increase.

But looking at things objectively, one has to reach the conclusion that today's youth just don't know how to cope with the world they're facing. Divorced parents, chaotic homes, lack of supervision and care, absence of sure standards, insecurity, and inability to trust others—all these things make the teenage world anything but a *young-only-once* paradise. Those who don't know Jesus face a world without hope. It's no wonder that escaping into alcohol, drugs, gambling, video games, gangs, and lots of other *less-than-healthy* alternatives appear attractive. So often there seems to be no way out.

Charles Stanley made a very interesting observation, with which I completely agree: "Listening to God and obeying Him are the only constructive methods that enable us to survive the storms of the twentieth century."[3]

Life is like a maze, in which every wrong turn brings peril and heartache. Only hearing God's voice and obeying it can keep you out of the serious trouble caused by unwise decisions.

Willingness to obey is a prerequisite for hearing "a word from the Lord." God knows everything. He knows whether or not you'll obey Him before He even communicates with you. Even though His mercy

[3] Charles Stanley, *Listening to God*, Nelson Audio Library, side 4.

and compassion often cause Him to warn you even if you're not ready to listen, He basically gives His directions only to those who are willing to follow them.

The devil works overtime making people afraid to obey God. Here are a few of his campaign slogans: "Christians don't have any fun." "If you really dedicate your life to God, He'll call you to be a miserable missionary." (I happen to know a lot of missionaries, and they're very happy and fulfilled people!) "Really spiritual people dress out of style and are so heavenly minded they're no earthly good." "If you stood up for Jesus at school, you'd lose all your friends." "She rededicated her life to the Lord two years ago and she hasn't had a date since."

To be honest with you, obeying God isn't always easy. Like the mother who serves vegetables instead of chocolates, God's priority is what is good for us—not what we want most. Just as the coach insists on rigorous training, which produces aching muscles and tired bodies, God concentrates on stimulating us to reach our full potential in Him—not on babying us and catering to our every desire. Instead of a self-centered comfort-zone existence, God challenges us to become agents of change in the world. It's a mind-blower, but God chose to depend on *us* for evangelizing the lost, comforting the hurting, and showing His love to people who need Him. You have to give up a lot to totally dedicate yourself to a cause, but it makes you a lot happier than being an unproductive couch potato!

I heard an interesting story on the radio the other day. One man decided that the quickest way to get rich was to discover uranium. He invested in a geiger counter and proceeded to explore a mountainous area, looking for the valuable mineral. Braving the elements, sometimes with insufficient funds to eat very well, he kept up the search for years. And he succeeded. He sold his claim for a fantastic sum, bought a mansion, retired early, and proceeded to live in luxury. However, he soon became bored and depressed, confiding that the happy years had been those in which he was trying to reach his goal. Now he felt that life had nothing exciting to offer anymore.

Jesus put it so well: "For whoever wants to save his life will lose it, but whoever loses his life for me will save it" (Luke 9:24) I'm convinced that He was referring to time as well as to eternity. The way to adventure, excitement, joy, and fulfillment is following God—even if, at times, the going gets tough. It's frustrating to be on the *nothing's-happened-yet-to-change-this-terrible-situation* side of a miracle. But when the Red Sea opens before you, there's nothing quite like it. Following God, and watching Him work in seemingly impossible circumstances is where it's at! You're a key person in the most important project in the history of the universe. Winning the world for Jesus is a crusade worthy of the best within you, a cause that will enable you to make a difference for all eternity.

Jesus said, "Blessed rather are those who hear the word of God and obey it" (Luke 11:28). God wants you to enjoy His very best. It's His will that you enter into marriage with no regrets, no shameful past you wish you could erase. He wants you to experience being used by Him to help someone choose heaven, seeing your prayers answered, sensing His peace in the midst of incredible chaos, and savoring the security of knowing what is right and what is wrong. *Obey* is a four-letter word—a very good one if God is the Person giving the orders.

Steps TO TAKE

1. Slowly, read Colossians 3 two times, asking God what steps of obedience He wants you to take in response to this Scripture.

2. Write down the things God instructs you to do and how you're going to go about implementing them. For example, "Lord, I need to clothe myself with humility" might mean telling your little brother that you were wrong and he was right about the distance of Mars from the sun, or it might require that you tell your English teacher you didn't really read the book you wrote your report on.

Other suggested passages for reading this way are: Romans 13; 1 Peter 5:5–11; 1 Thessalonians 5; and 1 Timothy 6:11–21.

Chapter Eleven
God, If I Were Running Your Universe

☞ First Impressions of What God Is Doing Can Be Deceiving
or
Lord, You Just Don't Fit Into the Cage I Made for You

Jason shuddered as he thought of entering the funeral home. That building had always seemed rather spooky to him. When he was younger, he and his friends told the usual humorous stories about caskets and death—but they had preferred to walk on the other side of the street. He always protested when his grandfather joked, "Some night I'm going to rent a room in that hotel." He had never wanted to see the inside of the place.

But now he had no choice. The events of the last thirty-six hours kept playing in his mind. Tuesday morning had started out just like any other. He and his best friend, Talon, met at his locker as usual to walk together to English class. They had laughed and joked, and Talon, who was the president of their church youth group, had excitedly shared his new plan for mailing an attractive evangelistic magazine to the home of every member of the senior class. Their small school boasted of ninety-six prospective June graduates. The magazine was expensive, but Talon had good fund-raising ideas.

After the usual boring grammar exercises, the bell rang and Talon had left for the band room with a cheerful, "I'll go through the lunch line first so I can save you a good seat." Those were the last words Jason ever heard from him.

As Jason was running up the stairs from the locker room after phys. ed, he heard shots and screams from the first-floor hallway. Mr. Miller, the gym teacher, ordered all students to leave the building. Amid pushing and shoving and mass hysteria, another shot rang out.

Everybody had shivered outside in the cold, fearing that something horrible had happened. The arrival of six police cars and two ambulances confirmed that suspicion. Four students were carried out on stretchers and, finally, Trevor Douglas, a drug pusher who had been expelled two years before, emerged in handcuffs, escorted by the police.

Eventually, students were ordered to return to their lockers to pick up their coats and to go home. Entering the building he knew so well gave Jason an eerie feeling. It was then he realized that Talon was no place in sight. He panicked.

Hurriedly, he had slipped into his jacket and run to Talon's house to tell his mom what had happened. The two of them decided to go check out the emergency room. His mom had scribbled a quick note: "Talon, we went to the hospital to see if you're okay. If you come home, please call Marysville to let us know you're safe." Then they jumped into the car and headed for the hospital in the next town.

When they arrived and asked for information at the desk, the receptionist explained that the four patients who needed immediate attention had absorbed the entire medical staff of the small hospital. There had been no time to identify the victims.

Talon's mother had insisted, "I'm Mrs. Jones. I'm expecting a telephone call from Talon Jones. Has it come through yet?"

"No one by that name has telephoned," the receptionist affirmed, "but I'll inform you if we receive the message."

They sat down on the blue plastic-covered chairs and began silently praying—panicky, incoherent prayers—at times fervent, at times interrupted by haunting uncertainties, at times remembering the others caught up in this nightmare. Each minute seemed like an eternity. And still there was no call from Talon.

Fifteen minutes later, Melinda Martin's parents arrived. Her mother was sobbing uncontrollably. "Emily saw Melinda get shot," her father explained. "We have no idea how serious it is."

"Margaret," Talon's mom ventured, "God is still in control. You can put your trust in Him. That will make things a lot easier."

"How can a loving God allow my innocent daughter to get shot within the walls of Central High?" the hysterical woman retorted. "I certainly don't want to hear anything about a supreme being."

Next came Barbara O'Keefe, Derek's mom. She was recently divorced and had just moved to Maple Grove. Derek was a very shy freshman, and Jason hardly knew him. "Do you have reason to believe that Derek may be one of the victims?" asked Mrs. Jones.

"Good reason," she answered. "Mrs. Banister called to tell me she was on hall duty and she saw Derek get shot in the leg."

"I'm so sorry," Talon's mother offered.

More people kept arriving—students, parents, and teachers—until there was standing-room only. As the clock ticked away and the tension mounted, less and less was said. Finally, two hours later, a very solemn-faced Dr. Hill appeared. "Usually I talk to families in private—but I think this horrendous event has made us all one big family, and we need to support one another. Nicole Meyers was shot in the arm, but her wound has been dressed and she should be okay. Derek O'Keefe's leg wound will require an operation and long recuperation, but he should suffer no long-term major problems. Melinda Martin is still unconscious, with a bullet lodged in her abdomen. She has been sent by ambulance to Ashton Hospital, where a specialist will assess her case and most likely operate.".

Some had burst into sobs, and Melinda's mother became hysterical.

When it was a little quieter, Dr. Hill continued. "I'm sorry we couldn't report to you sooner, but we were dealing with matters of life and death and our staff is very limited. Now—I regret to have to tell you that Talon Jones was shot in the chest and was pronounced dead on arrival...."

Now Jason replayed that horrible scene one more time as he followed his parents and his sister into the mortuary. He took a seat with them to wait until those who were not part of the immediate family could move forward and stand beside Talon's open coffin. When it came time, Jason wished he could run—but he had to face it. He put his arms around Talon's mom and dad and older brothers and then turned to the silent form of Talon—so stiff and cold and unresponsive.

All he could think was, "*Why?* Why Talon, God? He was the best Christian in school, and he planned to be a missionary. Why did you let him get shot?" And his own heart ached so much. How could he ever face going back to school or church without seeing Talon? Who would he study physics with? Who would he watch the World Series with? Who would he share his problems with? It didn't seem fair that God would allow him such intense emotional suffering.

Jason had always believed that the Lord knew what He was doing. The first table grace he'd learned started with, "God is great and God is good...." He'd never questioned God's justice before. But then, his life hadn't included any real tragedy. Now the question emerged with irresistible force—"Why would God allow such senseless loss of life?"

School was closed the day of Talon's funeral, which was held in the civic auditorium so everyone could attend. Talon's parents had invited a well-known youth evangelist, who was a friend of the family, to preach the sermon. At the end he gave an invitation, and thirty-five kids and two adults came forward. Jason determined to do all he could to follow them up and start the high school Bible study that Talon had always dreamed of.

That day, Jason realized something very important. We only see things from the earthly side, but God looks at circumstances through the binoculars of heaven. The only reason for us existing at all is to prepare for eternity, and sometimes even good and enjoyable things are swept aside to focus us on that purpose.

Although Jason still felt sad and shaken, his sense that we serve a God who knows what He is doing had returned. This time the Lord had permitted Jason to see something of a reason for permitting tragedy, and he was very grateful. Jason knew that this wouldn't always be the case.

Yet, he made a decision to trust that God's ways are higher than ours—even if we don't have a clue about God's purpose in the situation.

YOU HAVE AN APPOINTMENT WITH THE CREATOR OF THE UNIVERSE...
...to learn more about Him.

It Just Doesn't Seem Fair!

DAY 1

If you've ever been in a class where everybody got away with murder, you've seen injustice. Because the teacher refused to enforce the rules, bullies ran the show. Widespread cheating meant that those who really studied were treated unfairly. Besides this, the fun-and-games instructor who gave you what you wanted at the moment—no homework, no difficult exams, and a totally relaxing class hour—made you pay a terrible price later when you had to catch up on the material you never learned.

God is not like that teacher. His rules come with built-in consequences if they are disobeyed. Sex outside of marriage causes pain—to the illegitimate child, in the transmission of diseases, and in the form of inability to gain the trust of a marriage partner. A habitual liar has few friends. Refusal to listen to the wisdom of parents has resulted in many repeat performances of the prodigal son drama.

God knows it's not fair to permit Adolf Hitler to walk into heaven alongside the best Christian who ever lived. He has a system of rewards and punishments. But because His justice system includes both heaven and earth—and hell—and because it operates for both time and eternity, we don't always see the end result. Not every wrong will be righted immediately, but God knows what He's doing!

The Lord gives us what we need, not what we desire at the moment. Christians are to be soldiers in God's army—which means that advancing the cause of the kingdom of God is more important than the temporary comfort or emotional satisfaction of the individual soldier. In light of knowing we'll enjoy a forever with Him—and considering what He did on the cross to secure our salvation—we should be willing to suffer in His service. The refining process for gold, and for human character, requires some intense heat.

Since God is all-wise, we shouldn't complain the minute something *seems* to be unfair. Accepting the fact that God runs His justice system fairly gives you a lot of benefits—like peace of mind, comfort, joy, and the ability to sleep at night! Nehemiah understood this. Although his people were hurting and he was praying for relief, he told God, "In all that has happened to us, you have been just; you have acted faithfully, while we did wrong" (Nehemiah 9:33). When John saw the punishments against Christian killers, recorded in the book of Revelation, he gave this response: "Yes, Lord God Almighty, true and just are your judgments" (Revelation 16:7). As we recognize the validity of God's wrath, we should commit ourselves to doing everything possible to spread the gospel. In this way, we help limit the number of people who, for their rejection of God's plan of salvation, will experience the just judgment of God.

Steps
TO TAKE

1. Take some time to meditate on the following verses, memorizing one of them, and thanking God for His justice. In your own way, singing praises, making up a new song, or praying, worship your awesome and just God.

He is the Rock, his works are perfect and all his ways are just. A faithful God who does no wrong, upright and just is he. (Deuteronomy 32:4)

Righteous are you, O Lord, and your laws are right. (Psalm 119:137)

All your words are true; all your righteous laws are eternal. (Psalm 119:160)

Seven times a day I praise you for your righteous laws. (Psalm 119:164)

2. Experience an example of the justice of God by putting yourself in the place of Mordecai, who believed that it was wrong to bow down to anyone or anything except God. For his obedience to God, he found himself and his entire nation in big trouble.

Read Esther 3

How do you feel toward yourself, your enemies, and toward God when you find out you and your people are scheduled to be wiped out on December 13 (the thirteenth day of the last month Adar)? _____

_____

Read Esther 4:1–11

How do you react when Esther is afraid to approach the king because he might refuse to help her and have her killed? _____

_____

Read Esther 4:12–17

How do you feel when Esther asks you to organize a fast for all Jews to unite before God on her behalf as she prepares to approach the king? _____

_____

Read Esther 5

How do you feel when you hear about the gallows Haman has built to hang you on? _____

_____

Read Esther 6 and 7

How did you react when the king forced Haman to honor you? How do you feel now that Haman has been hanged on the gallows instead of yourself? _____

_____

Read Esther 8

How do you feel now that you have Haman's job and have reversed Haman's orders so that your entire nation will be saved? _____

_____

Back to the present

3. Write out what you think Haman might have prayed to God.

_____

4. When have you experienced God's justice? _____

_____

Remember that even though now you have an emergency similar to the one described in Esther, Chapter 3 or Chapter 5—accompanied by many fears and doubts—God plans to bring the situation to an Esther, Chapter 8 solution, either here or in heaven.

5. Spend some more time worshiping your just God—even thanking Him for the justice He plans for a presently unfair situation.

But Not Even Santa Claus Loves Everybody.

DAY 2

That we worship an amazingly merciful and compassionate God is provable just by reading the biography of a guy named Manasseh.

You may never have heard of this dude, but he was the son of Hezekiah, and he was a king of Judah. Although he had the advantage of a godly father and a good upbringing, he completely turned his back on the Lord. Not only did he worship idols, he brought statues of them into God's holy temple and sacrificed his sons as burnt offerings to them. Manasseh became deeply involved in witchcraft, consulting mediums and spiritists. He led the people of Judah astray until they were more pagan than those in the countries that surrounded them. God spoke to Manasseh and his nation—probably many times—but they paid absolutely no attention.

Finally, the king of Assyria ordered that a hook be put in Manasseh's nose, and that he be bound with chains, to be dragged to Babylon as a prisoner of war. Now, in his great misery, Manasseh asked God to help him. If you had been God, how would you have responded? After all, he deserved his situation.

The Lord not only forgave him but brought him again to Jerusalem and helped him to lead his people back to God. Manasseh is a monument to the mercy and love of God.

If somehow or other you've picked up the notion that God is super-critical, just waiting to come down on you the moment you do anything wrong, you'd better read your Bible more carefully. God is the God of a second chance—the God who forgives and forgets our sins, the God who longs to show you compassion.

The only requirement to receive His mercy is to chuck that *know-it-all* attitude and come humbly before Him, confessing your sin and determining to let Him call the shots from now on. Those who refuse to recognize their sinfulness are like the small child who accuses his mother of being unwilling to zipper his jacket while kicking so violently she can't even get near him! Such people insist that God is cruel and unfair as they continue to reject His great love and promise of a new and wonderful life. Open your heart to God and His mercy. God *does* love everybody, even if He's not some sentimental Santa Claus who does nothing but give out presents.

Steps TO TAKE

1. Reread the following verses until they become part of you, concentrating on phrases you can throw at the devil in the heat of combat. Repeat phrases like, "You are forgiving and good, O Lord," and, "But you, O Lord, are a compassionate and gracious God." When the devil tries to tell you that God has given up on you, take refuge in your all-merciful God and praise Him for His love.

But you, O Lord, are a compassionate and gracious God, slow to anger, abounding in love and faithfulness. (Psalm 86:15)

Give thanks to the Lord, for his love endures forever. (2 Chronicles 20:21)

For the Lord is good and his love endures forever; his faithfulness continues through all generations. (Psalm 100:5)

The Lord is gracious and compassionate, slow to anger and rich in love. The Lord is good to all; he has compassion on all he has made. (Psalm 145:8–9)

You are forgiving and good, O Lord, abounding in love to all who call to you. (Psalm 86:5)

For we do not have a high priest who is unable to sympathize with our weaknesses, but we have one who has been tempted in every way, just as we are—yet was without sin. Let us then approach the throne of grace with confidence, so that we may receive mercy and find grace to help in time of need. (Hebrews 4:15–16)

2. Experience God's love and care and mercy as you put yourself in the sandals of Elijah.

Read 1 Kings 17:1–16

What thoughts go through your mind when you know the king wants to kill you? _____

_____

What emotions battle within you when the brook dries up?_____

_____

How do you feel as you look back on how God provided for your physical needs of safety and food? _____

_____

Read 1 Kings 17:17–24
What doubts and fears plague you when you realize that the boy is dead? _____

_____

How do you feel after experiencing the miracle? _____

_____

Read 1 Kings 18
As Elijah, write in your diary, recording your intimate feelings about God. What is your response to the Mt. Carmel experience?_____

_____

Read 1 Kings 19:1–2
What is going on in your mind after receiving a death threat from Jezebel? _____

_____

Read 1 Kings 19:3–18
After this experience you pray to thank God for His love and His mercy. What do you say? _____

_____

Back to the present
3. Write a prayer of thanks for a time in your life when God showed you great compassion. _____

_____

4. Just spend some time thinking about the great love of God and how He's demonstrated that love to you. Worship the God of love and mercy!

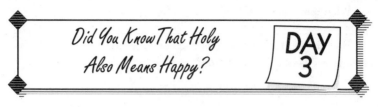

Did You Know That Holy Also Means Happy?

DAY 3

I remember reading Roman, Greek, and Norse mythology. The stories were good, but I was shocked to find gods and goddesses picking favorites, sleeping around, staging tantrums, and carrying out exaggerated schemes of revenge. It was horrifying to realize that some people actually worshiped such creatures.

How secure I felt that the God I serve is no Zeus, whose thunderbolts flew whenever he got ticked off. The God of the Bible obeys His own rules and He is perfectly holy.

The original meaning of *holy* is "sound, whole, and happy." Synonyms include perfect, pure, and untainted by evil or sin. God is all of these.

A rebellious society that loves to sin pictures holiness as something of a joke. Excitement, action, and popularity are equated with wrongdoing. Being nasty, aggressive, promiscuous, self-serving, and unwilling to submit to authority is considered the norm. Nobody considers the terms "goodie-goodie," "snitch," "holy joe," or "Jesus freak" as complimentary.

Because of this, today's Christians fail to appreciate the value of holiness. We seldom stand in awe of the holiness of God. Few people have an Isaiah experience in which the chorus "Holy, holy, holy, is the Lord Almighty; the whole earth is full of his glory" (Isaiah 6:3) is answered by "Woe to me!...I am ruined! For I am a man of unclean lips, and I live among a people of unclean lips, and my eyes have seen the King, the Lord Almighty" (Isaiah 6:5).

But as you contemplate the Person who never made a mistake, never had a bad attitude, never acted selfishly, and never thought anything He'd be ashamed of, you can catch that *God-is-in-heaven-and-you-are-on-earth-so-let-your-words-be-few* feeling of awe. Reflecting on His absolute purity will bring to mind some things you do that make you uncomfortable in His presence, and will give you a desire to change. Thinking of a flawless Being without sin should make you realize that you're approaching majesty, and it should transform your flippant *God-is-a-good-bud* mentality into one of respect and true adoration. "Ascribe to the Lord the glory due his name; worship the Lord in the splendor of his holiness" (Psalm 29:2). He's awesome, majestic, eternal, and without a single fault or blemish.

Bow before Him, kneel or fall on your face. He is worthy of all your adoration, all your reverence, and all your worship!

1. Meditate on these verses, repeating them over and over until you really digest their meaning. As you join those in heaven saying, "Holy, holy, holy is the Lord God Almighty, who was, and is, and is to come," your spirit will be lifted above geometry tests, scoldings from your mom, and an empty wallet.

Let them praise your great and awesome name—he is holy. (Psalm 99:3)

There is no one holy like the Lord; there is no one besides you; there is no Rock like our God. (1 Samuel 2:2)

Holy, holy, holy is the Lord God Almighty, who was, and is, and is to come. (Revelation 4:8)

"Great and marvelous are your deeds, Lord God Almighty. Just and true are your ways, King of the ages. Who will not fear you, O Lord, and bring glory to your name? For you alone are holy. All nations will come and worship before you, for your righteous acts have been revealed." (Revelation 15:3–4)

But the Lord is in his holy temple; let all the earth be silent before him. (Habakkuk 2:20)

But just as he who called you is holy, so be holy in all you do; for it is written: "Be holy, because I am holy." (1 Peter 1:16)

2. Put yourself in the place of a teenager who witnessed the giving of the Ten Commandments. Sense the holiness, majesty, and awesomeness of God.

Read Exodus 19:1–8
How did you react when you heard that if you and the other Israelites would obey God fully and keep His covenant (pact) you'd be His special people? _____

_____

Read Exodus 19:9–15
How did you feel when you put on your clean clothes and were told that anyone who touched the mountain from which a holy God was to reveal himself would be put to death?_____

_____
_____

What impression did all these preparations and instructions give you about the character of God?_____

_____
_____

Read Exodus 19:16–20:21
Why did you sense fear? _____

_____

Did you want to climb the mountain to get closer to God? Why or why not? _____

What things went through your mind as God spoke the Ten Commandments?_____

When many people were afraid to hear God speak again and Moses said, "God has come to test you, so that the fear of God will be with you to keep you from sinning," how did you feel?_____

Back to the present
Do you personally think of God as holy, majestic, and Someone *not* to mess around with—or is your "god" a namby-pamby who always lets you get your own way? _____

Do these two chapters change your concept of God? How? _____

3. Just meditate on the great holiness of God. Thank Him for His perfection, integrity, and unchanging character.

Choose the Right Security Blanket **DAY 4**

Do you really feel safe and secure? Your world may be caving in at this point, and you want to scream, "No!" But even if your dad's not in the process of marrying another woman, you don't have to change schools, and your grandmother didn't just die, you may sense that nothing seems very solid. You may be painfully aware that some international crisis thousands of miles away could change life as you know it. Because few people have any clear idea of right and wrong, you're probably meeting chaos and confusion almost everywhere. A diagnosis of cancer, a car accident, a job loss, a natural disaster, being betrayed by a friend—so many uncontrollable monsters loom on the horizon. The *poor-little-me-in-this-big-bad-world* refrain is a catchy little tune and rather easy to pick up.

There's an Ultimate Security Source, though—a Friend who will never let you let down, a Counselor who'll never give you a bum steer, a Comforter who will always understand. Your Creator will always be there for you if you'll take the time to form a deep relationship with Him. He won't die, or move away, or forget about you when someone more interesting comes along. He'll love you no matter what. He'll care enough to discipline you and tell you the truth. He'll keep on believing in you, even when everybody else gives up on you.

God always makes good on His promises. All of us know the pain of being let down. When people don't keep their word, we lose confidence. But God is different. You can depend on Him completely.

It's scary to see someone change right before your eyes. But it happens. After a year of heavy drug use, the guy you used to know has disappeared. Bitterness and unforgiveness can turn the once-cheerful parent into a grouch. Deteriorating health can alter a person beyond recognition. But God never changes. The investment you make in forming an intimate relationship with Him is a sound one. "Jesus Christ is the same yesterday and today and forever" (Hebrews 13:8).

The devil hates to see a secure Christian. He makes up all kinds of lies to keep you off balance and to torture you. He'll try to tell you that God doesn't love you anymore when you sin, when something terrible happens, or when you don't measure up to that standard someone else has set for you. But God shows His faithfulness even in nature—the sun comes up every morning, spring always follows winter, and there's an ecological balance that even man has a hard time destroying. People who have walked close to the Lord for many years all testify to the faithfulness of God—and some have lived through the most difficult of circumstances. The Lord won't let you down—no matter what.

The secret of security is to place all your hope in a God who never fails. If you expect of your parents what they are unable to give you, only disappointment and resentment await you. Placing your eyes on a Christian leader who may fall can set you up for a devastating experience. Friends are fickle and they often dissappoint you. Confiding in your good looks, your charm, or outstanding ability means that when others don't agree with your assessment of yourself, depression sets in. Your neat clothes, a place on the football or cheerleading squad, your wheels, or your spending money, might be gone tomorrow. Realize the risk of letting people or things be your security blanket. Instead, say with David: "When I am afraid, I will trust in you. In God, whose word I praise, in God I trust; I will not be afraid. What can mortal man do to me?" (Psalm 56:3–4). Claim the promise: "Whoever trusts in the Lord is kept safe" (Proverbs 29:25).

Steps TO TAKE

1. Reread these verses about God's faithfulness over and over until they become part of you. Choose your favorite and memorize it.

Your love, O Lord, reaches to the heavens, your faithfulness to the skies. Your righteousness is like the mighty mountains, your justice like the great deep. O Lord, you preserve both man and beast. How priceless is your unfailing love! Both high and low among men find refuge in the shadow of your wings. (Psalm 36:5–7)

It is good to praise the Lord and make music to your name, O Most High, to proclaim your love in the morning and your faithfulness at night. (Psalm 92:1–2)

I will sing of the Lord's great love forever; with my mouth I will make your faithfulness known through all generations. I will declare that your love stands firm forever, that you established your faithfulness in heaven itself. (Psalm 89:1–2)

Because of the Lord's great love we are not consumed, for his compassions never fail. They are new every morning; great is your faithfulness. (Lamentations 3:22–23)

2. Put yourself in the place of Gideon as you experience the faithfulness of God.

Read Judges 6:1–24

You are separating the husks from the wheat, which should be done in a high, windy place but you are hiding in a winepress—something like a very shallow well. Because of all the dust and chaff, your allergies are probably acting up. How do you feel when your pity-party is interrupted with, "The Lord is with you, mighty warrior"?_____

What questions plague you?_____

What doubts do you struggle with when the angel of the Lord commands you to save Israel from the Midianites? _____

Read Judges 6:25–32

Even though you're afraid to obey—and so you tear down Baal's altar at night—how does God demonstrate His faithfulness?_____

What reactions do you have as your father defends you? _____

Read Judges 6:33–40

After calling your countrymen to battle the Midianites, what emotions swell within you?_____

How does God again show His faithfulness, and how does that make you feel? _____

Read Judges 7:1–8

After obeying God, how do you feel about facing a huge Midianite army with 300 men? _____

Read Judges 7:9–15

What thoughts race through your mind as God once again demonstrates that He is totally trustworthy? _____

Read Judges 7:15–24

As you contemplate this great victory and the events that led up to it, how would you describe the God you serve? _____

Back to the present

Think about God's faithfulness to you. List some ways He has shown you that He will never leave you or forsake you. List them and thank Him that He's a faithful God. _____

_____

_____

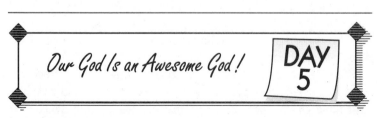

Our God Is an Awesome God! **DAY 5**

"Why doesn't God do something?"—about the famine that's taking so many lives, about the senseless killing evoked by hatred and greed, about the lady who assassinates with her tongue?

Certainly you've heard comments like this. Maybe you've even made them yourself.

It's not that God doesn't have the power to do whatever He wishes—it's that He has priorities more pressing than the momentary good His direct intervention could achieve. He created human beings with the ability to choose—good or evil. If He stepped in every time a person got out of line, that liberty would be a joke. He also ordained some automatic penalties for our disobedience to Him. And He doesn't prevent a sickness caused by our foolishness, neglect of our bodies, or promiscuity. He also permits tragedy, natural disasters, and trials designed to turn our minds toward the necessity of preparing for eternity. If horrible circumstances cause someone to accept Christ as Savior, that person is eternally grateful for the experience.

While God doesn't use His clout to remove every inconvenience or irritation from our existence, He stands ready to help His own loved children. "For the Lord your God is God of gods and Lord of lords, the great God, mighty and awesome, who shows no partiality and accepts no bribes. He defends the cause of the fatherless and the widow, and loves the alien, giving him food and clothing" (Deuteronomy 10:17–18). "Do not be terrified by them [gangs, mean teachers, kids who make fun of you, unfair bosses] for the Lord your God, who is among you, is a great and awesome God" (Deuteronomy 7:21). It is wonderful to know that an all-powerful God is on your side.

Have you ever watched blinding streaks of lightning, that make

Fourth of July fireworks look like peanuts—or been startled by a resounding clap of thunder? How about comparing the torrents of rain that fall from heaven with your puny sprinkling system? Don't the diamond rings in a jewelry store look pretty shoddy compared to the glistening droplets found on every leaf and flower and blade of grass if God decides to turn on the sun full blast after a shower? Add to that a breathtaking rainbow, and you have to admit that God can pull off some pretty amazing feats! A hurricane, a tornado, or an earthquake is an even more impressive show of strength.

The Lord can transform the alcoholic who used to beat his wife into a man of God, turn the gang leader into a preacher, and make the most timid girl in town into a dynamic witness for Him. When God starts working, the Red Sea opens, two small fish feed a multitude, the lame man leaps for joy, the atheist accepts Christ—and a Bible study group gets started at *your* high school!

The God of Elijah is your God. There are still "Queen Jezebels" who'd just as soon eradicate all Christians. The idols today aren't called baals—they have names like money, popularity, peer pressure, good grades, sports, social life, sex, and video games. There are still many "chameleon Christians" who only act born again at church. And like Elijah you may feel as if you're the only one who has opted for *24-hour-per-day* commitment. But the God you serve is Almighty. He can send fire from heaven, or make you strong enough to withstand temptation, or help you win your friends for Christ, or give you joy when you must stand alone for what is right. You never need to feel outnumbered, socially unacceptable, and discouraged. Our God is an awesome God!

1. Celebrate the strength and might of God—as well as the fact that you can plug in to His power. Meditate on each of these verses. Memorize them and take them with you wherever you go.

Ah, Sovereign Lord, you have made the heavens and the earth by your great power and outstretched arm. Nothing is too hard for you. (Jeremiah 32:17)

Yours, O Lord, is the greatness and the power and the glory and the majesty and the splendor, for everything in heaven and earth is yours. Yours, O Lord, is the kingdom; you are exalted as head over all. Wealth and honor come from you; you are the ruler of all things. In your hands are strength and power to exalt and give strength to all. (1 Chronicles 29:11–12)

Great is our Lord and mighty in power; his understanding has no limit. (Psalm 147:5)

You are awesome, O God, in your sanctuary; the God of Israel gives power and strength to his people. Praise be to God! (Psalm 68:35)

Then Jesus came to them and said, "All authority in heaven and on earth has been given to me. Therefore go and make disciples of all nations." (Matthew 28:18–19)

2. Imagine that you're an Israelite teenager when Moses appears on the scene in Egypt. Experience the great power of God.[1]

Read Exodus 5:1–21
What emotions do you have to deal with when you find out your father was beaten because Pharaoh became angry when Moses asked him to let God's people go? _____

_____

_____

Read Exodus 7:19–23; 8:5–6, 12–19
How do you feel about living through these four plagues? _____

_____

How do these events change your attitude toward God? _____

_____

_____

Read Exodus 8:22–24; 9:2–12
How does the fact that only the Egyptians suffer from these things make you rethink what it means to be one of God's chosen

---

[1]Putting yourself in the place of biblical characters as you read the Bible can give you insight on how to pray.

216

people? _____

What does it teach you about the character and power of God? ____
_____
_____
_____

Read Exodus 10:12–23

What did realizing that God could send grasshoppers and darkness, whenever and wherever He chose, do to your faith? _____
_____
_____

Read Exodus 12:1–13, 29–36

How do you feel about leaving Egypt and having your former slave-driver give you jewels, beautiful clothes, and other items of value? _____

As you look back on all that made this possible, how would you describe God? _____
_____

Read Exodus 14:1–12

What terrifying thoughts run through your mind as you see the best army in the world coming after you and that there is no escape route? _____
_____
_____

Read Exodus 14:12–31

Describe the sensation of passing through the Red Sea. _____
_____

What did you think when you saw the water fall back on the Egyptians? _____
_____

Write a little thank-you note to God for what He's done. _____
_____
_____

Back to the present
     How have you personally experienced God's power?_____
_____

_____

     If you'd trusted Him for more things, do you think you'd have seen
even more of His power? Give examples. _____
_____

_____

     3. Praise God for His mighty power.

Chapter Twelve
Out of Focus

Joel tried to shut out the buzz of his alarm clock. He didn't even want to get out of bed, much less face another day at school, go to football practice, or show up at Bible study. If only he could climb Mt. McKinley alone, take a plane to Siberia, or join some jungle tribe who'd never heard of a first down, a field goal, or an off-sides penalty!

But since he had no choice, he got ready for school, grabbed a bite of breakfast, and arrived at homeroom on time. Throughout the day, though, he tried to avoid everyone. And during Mr. Berg's boring history lecture, he again relived the disaster that so made him want to escape....

Joel, as a junior, had aced out Mike MacIntosh as first-string quarterback. After three wins in a row, he'd become an instant hero. But that was before Friday night's game against Jefferson High, a school with an average team, which West expected to defeat with ease. First, Joel made a touchdown pass—to Jefferson High's right end! In possession of the ball again, Joel fumbled and their opponents recovered. Behind 14-0, West started the fourth quarter with their power play—but Joel was sacked for a fifteen-yard loss. They had to punt, and Jefferson brought the ball down field until it was within four yards of a touchdown. And it was Joel who drew a penalty for unnecessary roughness, which so demoralized the team that Jefferson easily made another TD.

At this point, the coach put Mike in—even though he was just recovering from the flu—and he played very well.

Newspaper headlines called the game the upset of the year, and the article sarcastically commented that Joel Martinez was by far the most valuable player—as far as Jefferson was concerned. The coach bawled him out, the guys got on his case, and even Tiffany commented, "Joel, you really messed up. What happened?"....

Joel felt like a total failure. He couldn't stop reliving his errors long enough to concentrate on history, or to listen to his coach's instructions, or to pray. He even had nightmares about being tackled by NFL players wearing Jefferson uniforms.

He arrived at Bible study without his Bible and in no mood to hear a pep talk. But Tom, ever enthusiastic and thoroughly convinced that God can handle anything, realized that something was wrong. "Before we start our study," he began, "I'd like to share with you a secret I've learned.

"When I was your age, I was always down on myself and could

become depressed over things like the appearance of a new zit, a girl who wouldn't smile at me in the hall, or dropping my books as I boarded the school bus. Finally, one day, my grandfather told me, 'Tom, you think an awful lot about yourself, and so little about God. Who's really more important in this universe—you or God?'

"That caught me by surprise," said Tom. "What he said was true. Then my grandfather—who was always cheerful, even though he faced a lot of difficult circumstances—gave me some of the most important advice I've ever received. He said, 'When you get discouraged with yourself, concentrate on God. You'll never be disappointed with Him. And if you look at things from His point of view, there won't be anything to be depressed about. The apostles rejoiced because they were counted worthy to suffer for their wonderful Savior and that they'd receive big prizes in heaven. If you started to think about God's plans and activities rather than your own, Tom, things would change.'

"You know, I took that counsel to heart," Tom concluded. "And my life hasn't been the same since."

In spite of his determination to stay depressed, Joel couldn't help hearing what Tom had to say. Instead of paying attention to the Bible study, he thought of Tom's words. Finally, when Joel did tune in, Tom was closing.

"Praising God beats pity-partying any day. Tonight we're going to go around the circle a few times, and each guy has to express something to praise God for."

Greg, who was kind of a goof-off, made everyone laugh by starting, "I praise God that I only have to spend forty-three minutes a day in Ms. Campbell's class."

When it came Joel's turn, he nonchalantly chirped, "I praise God that He didn't paint the sky fluorescent orange." But finally the group ran out of jokes and began to praise God for real things like—"helping me study just the right material for Tuesday's geometry test," "supplying the money for me to go on the ski retreat," and, "convincing my father that I could continue to attend this Bible study."

In spite of everything, Joel did start thinking about God and all *He* has done. Although he didn't say it out loud, he thought, *I thank God that once I get to heaven I won't remember that football game anymore.*

Next he thought of how God gave Jonah a second chance. Maybe prophets and quarterbacks have something in common. He hoped so. Then he remembered what God did for Joshua when he made a super big mistake. Joshua, fooled by the first masquerade party in history, signed a peace treaty with his pagan neighbors—totally against God's orders. His popularity rating plummeted. But within a short time God gave him a tremendous victory and even answered his prayer that the sun stand still in order to complete defeating the enemies.

Hope started to replace despair. Joel began to see how thinking about what God *has* done, and *can* do, was a lot better than rehashing what he had done or should have done. For the first time in his life he began to see what "praising God" was all about. God created us to praise Him, and we can't function properly if we fail to do it. Joel realized that his self-centered thoughts had gotten him completely out of focus, but putting his mind on God was helping him to see things a lot more clearly.

YOU HAVE AN APPOINTMENT WITH THE CREATOR OF THE UNIVERSE... ...to learn to praise the God who gives your life meaning.

Have You Told God Lately That You Like His Landscaping?

DAY 1

Although it's true that "the heavens declare the glory of God; the skies proclaim the work of his hands" (Psalm 19:1), there's a lot being done to try to hide that fact. Instead of permitting students to appreciate the greatness of the God who paints leaves gold and orange and scarlet each fall and installs intricate timing devices in migrating ducks so they know when to fly south each year, biology books hint that every plant and animal and person evolved without the aid of an intelligent Creator. Taking good care of the planet God entrusted to us for our use and enjoyment has been replaced by a reverence for "mother earth," and by attempts to be aligned with the mysterious forces of nature. Once again in world history, there is an epidemic of, "They exchanged the truth of God for a lie, and worshiped and served created things rather than the Creator—who is forever praised" (Romans 1:25).

The conviction that everything, including your own existence, was only an accident robs you of purpose and destiny—and any reason to do what's right. The belief that "god is in everything and everything is part of god" blurs the distinction between Creator and created things. If "god" is reduced to your own dimensions—a person who must blow his or her nose, a being that forgets all about play practice on Tuesday afternoon, and an entity that freaks out when the line is still busy, then there's certainly no hope on the horizon. If the vulture that looks for dead dinners, the mosquito that spoils your picnic, and the cockroach that has yet to make a human friend should be objects of our worship because they are part of "god," then it would seem rather impossible to admire the characteristics of this "god."

However, the truth is that God is our Creator. "His creation came from the resources of His own infinite being, which was always here. When we say He makes things 'out of nothing,' we mean that He does not need any resource external to himself, does not lose part of himself in creating, and that His creation is distinct from himself rather than an extension of His being."[1] He is above His creation, and He has authority over it. He has made a rational, predictable universe in which the book you throw out the window never sprouts wings to fly upward.

---

[1] W. A. Pratney, *The Nature and Character of God* (Minneapolis: Bethany House Publishers, 1988), p. 134.

The earth doesn't change orbit and get so close to the sun that all Idaho produces instant fried potatoes, and water doesn't suddenly begin to freeze at 60° Fahrenheit, wrecking everybody's car radiator. Because God is a consistent rational Being, His creation reflects it.

God's creation is meant to give us a special appreciation for the Master Designer: "For since the creation of the world, God's invisible qualities—his eternal power and divine nature—have been clearly seen, being understood from what has been made, so that men are without excuse" (Romans 1:20). And unless you're blinded by false teaching, running from God, or so caught up in yourself that you notice nothing else, seeing a thundering waterfall, watching a playful kitten, or trying to count the stars in a night sky automatically gives you a desire to praise the God who made all these amazing things. A trip to the doctor's office occasioned just because one tiny part of your body is malfunctioning should make you appreciate the Genius who planned such a complex organism, capable of so many incredible processes.

If you don't notice the glory of your Maker in the beauty of a sunrise over a crystal-clear lake, the majesty of a snow-capped mountain, the vastness of a desert landscape, or the velvet softness and fragrance of a single red rose, then you're missing out on one of life's greatest pleasures. Walking with God and sensing His presence in a forest of stately pine trees, on the wave-flattened sands of an ocean beach, or exploring the muffled shadows so beautifully blurred together by the morning fog is to experience a captivating closeness with Him.

It's neat to be able to join in the ecstacy of broadcasting: "The Lord reigns, let the earth be glad; let the distant shores rejoice.... His lightning lights up the world; the earth sees and trembles. The mountains melt like wax before the Lord, before the Lord of all the earth" (Psalm 97:1, 4–5).

When you recognize God as great and good and Creator of everything, you feel fantastic inside—like you're flowing with the right current. Not only does praising God for His creation help you, it's important to God.

You're not too happy when others take everything you do for granted, failing to notice your originality—right? Maybe God would appreciate some complimentary comments from you on His creativity! After all, His landscaping is pretty outstanding!

Steps TO TAKE

1. Carefully read Psalm 104, praising God for all the things He has made.

2. Then compose your own psalm of praising the Lord for His wonderful workmanship displayed in nature. You might do this by making up your own song—either written or extemporaneous, praying your thanks for "all things bright and beautiful, all creatures great and small." Or you could come up with a formal written psalm, using either prose or poetry.

The important thing is that you give Him your heartfelt appreciation for the world He fashioned—especially for you.

A Ferris Wheel, Adolf Hitler, and Meaning in Life

DAY 2

So many ancient people viewed time as an ever-turning wheel, with no beginning and no end—existence without destination. And you do have to admit that a lot of human actions are repeated over and over again. You go to bed so that you can get up every morning, only to fall asleep at the end of each day. You eat a hamburger and then get so hungry you can gobble down a medium-sized pizza in a couple minutes—and soon your stomach is demanding ice cream. If you clean your room it gets dirty again, and if you wash clothes this week, you'll soon discover that the job must be done once more. One generation replaces another—the baby grows up, it's mother becomes an older woman, and the grandmother dies. Soon the baby is the mother and the mother turns into the grandmother. If one didn't know better, these endless cycles suggest meaninglessness.

But there is one fact that changes all this. God is at work in history—and in each individual life. The human situation isn't one vicious Ferris wheel, which never goes anywhere and never means anything and never stops. There was a definite starting point: "In the beginning

God created the heavens and the earth" (Genesis 1:1). He made Adam and Eve—and everyone else—in His own image with the purpose to "fill the earth and subdue it" (Genesis 1:28), and "to share in the inheritance of the saints in the kingdom of light" (Colossians 1:12).

The Bible teaches that Jesus will come to close out history, and John seeing this in a vision described the future scene: "And books were opened. Another book was opened, which is the book of life. The dead were judged according to what they had done as recorded in the books" (Revelation 20:12).

Because "man is destined to die once, and after that to face judgment" (Hebrews 9:27), each day of your life counts for eternity. The wonderful thing about your existence is that God sent Jesus to die for you so that by accepting Him as Savior, you can be assured of a forever with Him that is more fantastic than anything you could ever imagine.

What happens on the international scene also has meaning. God called Assyria "the rod of my anger" because He used that cruel and conquering country to punish the idol-worshiping people of Israel. Hardhearted Pharaoh brought glory to God by providing a context for God's marvelous miracles. Scripture mentions famine, war, natural disaster, and disease as warnings, which turn the minds of people from daily trivia to the Lord who made heaven and earth, causing them to turn from indifference and wrongdoing to repentance and faith.

What happens has meaning. It's not always discernible from the human side, but it makes a lot of sense when viewed from a heavenly perspective. It took a terrible earthquake in Mexico City to make my friend decide to accept Christ—and it shook up a lot of people enough so they came to know Jesus.

"Okay, I'll concede that," you might be saying. "But could anything good really come out of something as devastating and heartbreaking as World War II?"

And the answer is *yes.* Adolph Hitler's destruction of six million Jews so rallied world sympathy that the United Nations voted into existence the nation of Israel, a direct fulfillment of a seemingly impossible prophecy. Many soldiers, seeing firsthand the conditions in under-evangelized nations, dedicated their lives to missionary service. The pilot who led the attack on Pearl Harbor and who would never have had a chance to hear the gospel in an unoccupied Japan later became a Christian. A German concentration camp challenged the Christian commitment of Corrie ten Boom, and a Holland under Nazi control gave Brother Andrew—then a teenager—a free course in courage, that has made his ministry possible. Actually, a few books could be written on the subject.

All history is a monument to biblical truth: "Righteousness exalts a nation, but sin is a disgrace to any people" (Proverbs 14:34). "Blessed is the nation whose God is the Lord" (Psalm 33:12). When people forget God, their nation is plagued by problems, but when they repent of their sins and wholeheartedly return to the Lord, the country benefits.

The story of the Jewish people recorded in the Bible bears this out. Nations changed for the better as a result of the Wesleyan revival in England, the Welsh awakening in 1904, and even the U.S. "Jesus Revolution" of the 1970s. But when people turn their backs on God and popularize sin, conditions worsen. The fall of the Soviet Union is a good modern-day example, one the Western world would do well to heed. All this should lead thinking people to the conclusion that preparing to meet God is the most important thing they can do in this life. It should also cause you to praise the God who works in history.

"So what does this all mean for me?" you ask.

I'll tell you. First of all, it signals that you should look for God's hand in current events—not only for signs which indicate that Jesus will soon return but for direction in praying for certain leaders and situations, and for confirmation of your belief that sooner or later God punishes wrongdoing. Also, when things look dismal, it's good to review the past track record of how the prayers of God's saints have changed impossibilities. Here's a faith builder from the pen of Brother Andrew:

"Back in 1983 our [missionary] organization, Open Doors, called for seven years of prayer for the Soviet Union. We were convinced that the evil conspiracy that had brought untold misery and torment to the Body of Christ worldwide was headquartered in one place: Moscow ... Within a year we began to see results. We heard for the first time about an obscure man named Gorbachev.... The winds of change we prayed for began to blow, and there was no holding them back. Finally, just under six years from the time we first began praying, the walls between East and West began to crumble. The Berlin Wall—a worldwide symbol of Communist oppression—came tumbling down. Prison doors began to open. Eastern Europe rose up against the powers that had held them in bondage. In 1989, after more than thirty years of smuggling Bibles behind the Iron Curtain, I challenged the Russians openly to allow our organization to distribute a million Russian-language Bibles to Soviet churches. Incredibly they said yes."[2]

And this miracle is still progressing. *How about praying instead of complaining* about your country's problems!

Finally, remember that the God who works in history has a special purpose for each person. You are not some poor soul being endlessly reincarnated in some cycle of *karma*, being punished for things you did in some past life of which you're totally unconscious, and looking forward only to becoming a blob of nothingness in outer space somewhere. Your life was specifically designed by a loving and personal God who has woven meaning into every moment. You're doing things that matter and going places—most important, you're preparing to travel to the place where "he will wipe every tear from their eyes. There will be no more death or mourning or crying or pain, for the old order of things has passed away" (Revelation 21:4). And your trip will be more exciting if you learn to praise the God of history.

Steps TO TAKE

1. Carefully read Psalms 106 and 136, reliving the marvelous deeds of a God who works in history, a God who remains faithful despite the foolish choices, indifference, and sinful actions of His people.

2. Then list some things you know or have experienced about God intervening in the human story. For example: The delegates to the Constitutional Convention were deadlocked, but after taking a three-day prayer recess they worked out their differences. Or—my brother Johnny should have been killed in that car wreck, but God saved his life.

3. Then spend some time praising God that He's in control of all history—especially the news reports that make you uneasy. Also pray, as God leads you, for some tense world situations, knowing that by praying you're doing something to impact current events.

---

[2] Brother Andrew, *And God Changed His Mind* (Grand Rapids: Baker, 1991).

Memories Should Be Made Of This | DAY 3

It happens to everyone—the big disappointment. The guy or girl you like starts dating someone else; you had your heart set on a car, but now you know the cost of the insurance premium; an operation means that your dream of breaking some records for your school in your sport can no longer be realized. Or maybe it's a family crisis. Your sister is running off with some drug addict, or your father just lost his job. Possibly it's personal—like not being accepted by the group, having a learning disability, or never measuring up to your mother's expectations.

Whatever lies behind it, your discouragement deepens into depression—nothing seems to matter, nobody really understands. You feel trapped and forgotten. What should you do?

In Psalm 42 and 43, you can learn how David handled such feelings. He started out not by deciding that everything was hopeless or detailing the problem but by realizing that what he needed was more of God. This is always David's bottom line: To get through a crisis, I must have more of the power of the Holy Spirit in my life. However, there was also the emotional dimension. David admitted when he was really down, and told the Lord when others were making fun of him and asking, "Where is your God now?"

But then he remembered past victories in his spiritual experience. He recalled how he joined everybody else in praising God and the joy they shared. It put his mind back on what God *can* do. Even though he vacillated back and forth, the thing that gave him hope was placing his thoughts back on God and His faithfulness.

When trials come, it's a good idea to spend time thinking about the day you accepted Christ, to reflect on answers to prayer, to relive the times He rescued you from danger, and to meditate on all the blessings you've received. Like David, you can learn to gently steer your mind back to what God has done in the past.

Where might you be right now and what might you be doing if you'd never accepted Jesus as Savior? It's kind of frightening to even ponder this, but it will also cause you to praise and thank Him for all

He's done for you. What might your present problem be if you *didn't* know God? Realize that He can help you the same way in the future as He has in the past.

Memories, like so many facets of life, can be used for good and for evil. You've probably listened to the elderly lady who doesn't miss a beat as she recounts how fifty years ago her scoundrel of a boyfriend deceived her into thinking he was planning to marry her, and then eloped with her best friend. Or the man who insists on telling anyone who will listen how his life has been filled with one misfortune after another. For some people, the past can serve as an escape from present reality. There are people who spend their whole lives replaying the high point of their existence—the honor awarded, the feat accomplished, or the job landed by acing out 250 qualified applicants. It's a way of forgetting the here and now. Some people just stuff their recollections because remembering is too painful.

But God can give a totally different dimension to memories. He can heal those that are hurtful. And He can use the rest to show you His faithfulness in caring for your needs and rescuing you from the pitfalls brought on by pessimism, promiscuity, and pride. How many times did God put someone in your path with just the needed warnings or the perfect word of encouragement? Can't you think of times when the Lord provided exactly what you needed at just the right moment? Has God ever supernaturally protected you from harm? Meditating on these *miniature miracles* can build your faith in a God who can do for you today and tomorrow what He did yesterday and the day before.

"Great are the works of the Lord; they are pondered by all who delight in them. Glorious and majestic are his deeds" (Psalm 111:2–3). Memories should be made of this!

Steps TO TAKE

1. Carefully read Psalm 42 and 43, filling in these boxes as you go along.

Psalms 42 and 43	
Practicing Positive Self-Talk	*Projecting a Correct View of God*
What does David ask himself and what does he tell himself?	List all David's descriptions of God.
Expecting God to Intervene	*Looking beyond the Present*
What does David pray for?	What Does David say about his future?

2. Reread the two psalms, filling in anything you missed the first time.

3. Make a list of the times God has specifically helped you, His special blessings, and His daily faithfulness. Keep it, so you can look at it and focus your mind on memories of God's goodness on days you tend to feel depressed.

Note: You can make simple charts like this one to better capture what the Bible teaches about God so you can pray more effectively.

Hanging Around With Heroes

DAY
4

Reading through the Psalms, one soon notices how often the author's praise of God leads him to recall the miracles that are part of the history of Israel. Remembering the incredible deeds of the Almighty, which are all part of the majestic panoramic plan to bring salvation to man, inspires awe and admiration. If Joseph hadn't forgiven and saved his family, they all would have starved to death and the tribe of Judah destined to bring Jesus into the world would have been wiped out. If Esther hadn't petitioned for her people, the Jews would have disappeared from the face of the earth, and no descendant of David could have given birth to a Savior. Saying that history is His Story is no exaggeration, and studying biblical miracles is a real faith booster.

It's become an automatic habit with me: Whenever a situation seems impossible, I open my Bible to an account that tells how God changed some mountain into a mole hill. Once, I turned to Exodus 14, relived the dramatic escape of the Israelites, and almost experienced their terror as they looked back and saw Pharaoh's great army marching after them! Some words leaped off the page to speak to my present situation: "The Egyptians you see today you will never see again" (Exodus 14:13). God was undoubtedly tired of hearing my tale of woe concerning the "Egyptians" in my life. I saw things in a new light, and although the situation didn't change immediately, my distress was gone. A little later, things took a dramatic turn for the better.

When the work load seems overwhelming, I read about Nehemiah and the Jews rebuilding the wall of Jerusalem. I once again focus on the winning combination of prayer, persistence, refusing to listen to satanic lies, and obedience to God. It always gives me a new perspective on my present project. If I feel like a small and insignificant individual facing insurmountable odds, I turn to the story of David and Goliath. Again, I realize that "one with God is a majority."

Afraid to obey God's instructions, I read about Gideon who was also a scaredy-cat with a strong desire to follow God. The result of his obedience, regardless of the emotional battle, gives me some much-needed courage.

I find 2 Chronicles 20 my all-time favorite. King Jehoshaphat learned that a strong enemy alliance had come to fight his little army. He led the nation in prayer and fasting, using the spiritual strategy of sending the choir singing praises to God in front of the soldiers. The Lord caused these invaders to begin fighting one another, and the Israelites had only to celebrate their glorious victory. Shortly after really studying this passage, I found myself on the side of a highway far from anyone who could help, with my ignition keys locked in my trunk. I thought of Jehoshaphat, and that made me really expect God to rescue me. I sat down by the road to pray. Within minutes a very polite gentleman driving a tow truck asked if I needed help. I explained the situation and he promised to send someone from the gas station. After a while another man appeared and quickly opened my trunk. All of a sudden my praise party was interrupted with the realization that I had only ten dollars in my purse. Hesitantly I asked, "How much do I owe you?" The guy smiled and answered, "Two bucks." To me, this miracle was just as great as Jehoshaphat's military victory.

Faced with the possibility of laws I may not be able to go along with, I remember Shadrach, Meshach, and Abednego's deliverance from the fiery furnace and Daniel in the lions' den. I want to be like them. Right now there are some Jerichos in my life, but it's neat to know that God can knock down these walls as easily as He did in the time of Joshua. The God who surrounded Elisha with angelic forces, who pulled off an earthquake to release two of his servants from prison, and who fed five-thousand people with five loaves and two fishes can certainly take care of me!

"For everything that was written in the past was written to teach us, so that through endurance and the encouragement of the Scriptures we might have hope" (Romans 15:4). And not all of God's mighty deeds recorded in the Bible, which make it easier for us to trust God, remain in the past. Some spill over into the present. We should constantly praise God for giving His Ten Commandments and inspiring the writing of His holy Word. Where would we be without these divine instructions? The fact that Jesus rose from the dead affects us every day we live. He's at the right hand of God the Father, praying for us! Because He conquered death, we don't need to fear it. Hanging around with heroes of the faith—Moses, Joshua, Elijah, Gideon—is a really good idea. It draws your attention to their miracle-working God who, by the way, is still in business today!

Steps
TO TAKE

1. As you read Psalm 105 and Psalm 111, really praise God for His miracles.

2. Which biblical miracle is your favorite? Why? _____

_____

3. On a separate sheet of paper try writing a psalm of praise based on that event, adding as David does in Psalm 106 a few of God's other fantastic feats.

4. Develop a miracle mentality by meditating on what God has done and anticipating what He will do.

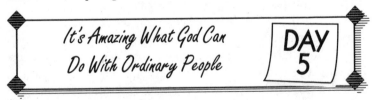

It's Amazing What God Can Do With Ordinary People

DAY 5

"That's just the way I am, and I can't act any differently." "It's useless to try to reform him so just accept him the way he is." "You can't change human nature."

We say things like that a lot. And it's obvious that most attempts to alter basic personal behavior have failed. In spite of educational emphasis on equality and respect for people of all backgrounds, racial hatred seems to be growing. All the information available on the harm done by drugs, cigarettes, and alcohol doesn't dissuade young people from using them. Neither prisons nor chemical-dependency programs seem to have much success in improving those under their care. No matter how much is written about the futility and horror of war, modern armies are as barbaric as any in history.

But there is hope—because the amazing power of Jesus Christ can totally transform lives! It's exciting to read how a Saul of Tarsus dedicated to destroying Christians got converted and became one of the most motivated missionaries of all time. The wimpy Peter, who denied that he even knew Jesus, later preached unashamedly to a huge crowd, which possibly contained some of the same people who heard his denials. James and John, whose quick tempers gave them the nickname "sons of thunder," turned into men whose lives reflected more and more of their humble Savior. John is now known as the "apostle of love."

Jesus can change anybody. He can change you.

Biographies of Christians whom the Lord has used in a special way point to the greatness of God. Someone is reported to have attended a meeting where D. L. Moody, a famous evangelist of the last century, was preaching. He commented that there was no relationship between the man behind the pulpit and what occurred that night. It was just that God chose to display His power through a simple and uneducated ex-shoe salesman who had completely surrendered his life to God.

Maybe you've never heard of J. O. Fraser, but his story is fascinating. Giving up everything, he went to China as a missionary. And after serving in other areas, he felt God wanted him to evangelize the Lisu people who lived in the mountains. For ten years, he worked and prayed and got many others to pray for these primitive demon-worshipers. But the idea of stopping their ancient practices filled them with terror. That Fraser could be content with Christ alone—even though deprived of all contact with other Christians and people of his intellectual level, all the while living in the most primitive conditions, with tribesmen totally indifferent to his message—is one of God's special miracles. Making what he thought would be his final visit to the villages before transferring to a different missionary station, Fraser saw family after family—400 in all!—make solid commitments to Christ.

"Oh, the depth of the riches of the wisdom and knowledge of God!

How unsearchable his judgments, and his paths beyond tracing out!" (Romans 11:33). Hearing about how God works makes us want to praise and adore Him more.

Gladys Aylward, who was employed as a servant girl in England, offered herself to a mission board to serve in China. She was rejected because it was thought her lack of formal education would keep her from learning the difficult Chinese language. Undaunted, she took a train across Russia all by herself and miraculously found the lady missionary she had come to help. When her companion died, Gladys told the Lord how terribly lonely she was. He started sending her orphans—and not only did she raise them to be strong Christians, she never felt lonely again. During the Japanese invasion of China, God showed Gladys just when to lead the children to safety. This was so noticeable that when Gladys moved her children to a different town, many people followed her, rightly assuming that the city she just left was about to fall to the Japanese. That God uses availability, not ability, is amply demonstrated in this story of His faithfulness.

Reading biographies of people who fully followed God is a most uplifting and enjoyable pastime. Try it. It'll cause you to praise the God who worked so wonderfully in the lives of other people.

Another faith-builder is watching God change you and the people you know. Not long ago, a guy came to our youth meeting all excited. A former gang member, he'd been assaulted as he'd left his home for church. He couldn't believe how much God had changed him, because instead of a desire to get even, God put into his heart a love for his assailant.

Do *you* know some former alcoholics and drug addicts who are now serving God? I do. In your church, are there some couples whose marriages were on the rocks before they came to know the Lord of love, who renewed in them genuine affection for each other? There are in mine. A few young people are growing so fast, one can almost measure their progress from week to week.

If you're serious about God, you'll be able to point to changes He's made in you! It's boring to be "saved, sanctified, and *petrified*." God wants to show off His talent for remodeling personalities, using you as an example! A *you're-the-Potter-I'm-the-clay* attitude toward your Maker will allow miracles to become the rule rather than the exception in your life.

Steps TO TAKE

Let's look at how God changed Peter. Be sure to carefully read each Scripture passage because this study can be of help to you personally. It will lead you to give thanks to the Savior who can do so much to alter the course of a life God wants to use without destroying the basic human personality. Under His control, even our weaknesses can be transformed into characteristics He'll use for His glory.

Put the emphasis on God, not on yourself. Ask Him to do for you what He did for Peter, and praise Him all during the process. The reason the Lord could work in Peter was that He was available. In spite of his failures, his heart's desire was to follow God. Why don't you tell God you want to be another Peter, and start thanking Him now for what He will do in your life?

1. Learn about God's life-changing power by studying the life of Peter. God even used Peter's big mouth. Lips that once talked before thinking (Luke 9:28–36), later delivered a sermon after which three thousand people were saved (Acts 2:1–41)! Peter's sometimes-impulsive initiative, that got him out of the boat and walking on water (Matthew 14:25–31) compelled him to cut off the ear of the high priest's servant when Jesus was arrested (John 18:1–11) and made him run to the tomb to check out the reports of women (Luke 24:9–12). Nonetheless, he was fine-tuned by the Holy Spirit into a wise and dynamic leader (Acts 1:15–26; 3:1–26; 9:32–43; 8:14–25).

The independent and proud Peter boasted that he'd always be loyal to Jesus even though nobody else was (Matthew 26:31–35), and he was not slow to tell even Jesus what to do (Matthew 16:13–28). But he became a man who was willing to listen to others when he needed to be set straight. Combining Galatians 2:11–16 with Acts 15:1–12, we can realize that Peter defended Paul, who had once corrected him in public for acting hypocritically!

The man who used to sleep through prayer meeting (Mark 14:32–38) learned to use every spare moment to communicate with

God (Acts 10:1–48). The guy who had an opinion about everything (John 13:3–11) was now so open to listening to God that the Lord gave him supernatural knowledge (Acts 5:1–11). The disciple who once thought he'd return to fishing (John 21:1–23) now preached the gospel whenever and wherever he could (Acts 5:29–32). Peter, who had been so afraid that He denied Jesus three times in a row (Mark 14:66–72), became so bold that he testified in front of all the Jewish leaders (Acts 4:1–22). And he was so willing to give his life for Jesus that he slept soundly the night before his scheduled execution (Acts 12:1–19).

Peter, transformed by the power of the Holy Spirit (Acts 2:1–13; 4:31), had the power to proclaim that the crucified Savior was alive (Acts 2:22–24) and the willingness to obey God no matter what it cost (Revelation 12:11).

2. If *you* want to have a powerful reason to praise God, ask Him to overhaul your personality. And praise Him as you watch Him work!

☑ Congratulations! You Finished the Book!

You've worked through a lot of different prayer possibilities. Use the ones that helped you most—and if you feel like you're in a rut, refer to this book again and try something else. And most important, decide that getting to know God better will always be a priority in your life.